Dark Passages

A Mystery Thriller in Two Acts

by
Shannon Michal Dow, Jan Henson Dow & Robert Schroeder

Popular Play Service

Bluffton, S.C.

Procedures & Policies ☎ Popular Play Service

33 Candlelight Lane, Bluffton, S.C. 29909

e-mail: popplays@hargray.com

Obtaining Examination Copies:

Playbooks may be purchased through our offices. Please contact us for list price plus current rates for postage and handling charged in the U.S. and outside the U.S.

Royalty Procedures and Policies:

Contact us for royalty rates for amateur productions of our full-length plays and for one-act plays with average attendance under 400 per performance, for amateur productions playing to higher average attendance per performance, and for rates applying to professional productions.

Playbooks must be purchased for each cast member and the stage manager and director.

When new plays are offered in manuscript (8-1/2 x 11" pages in report covers), permission to make copies for production purposes only, from the script initially provided, is granted for a flat fee. Conatact us for rates.

Rights to produce our plays when granted include the right to reproduce the play's title logo for advertising or for programs.

Royalties are payable two weeks in advance of the first performance. Royalties must be paid for every performance before an audience, whether or not admission is charged.

General Provisions:

No television, film, video or audio recording may be made of your production at any time.

It is an infringement of the copyright to copy part or all of our manuscripts or playbooks by any means.

It is an infringement of the copyright to give any public performance or reading of our plays either in their entirety or in excerpts without the prior consent of Popular Play Service.

Authorization to perform our plays when granted is predicated on the following conditions: (a) the title may not be altered; (b) there may be no deletions, alterations or changes of any kind to the script; (c) proper authorship credit must be given in all programs and all advertisements; and (d) the program must include the following statement, "Produced by special arrangement with Popular Play Service."

CAST: (In order of appearance)

Harold Lemb: 30 to 40 years old – usually reserved and secretive and, at times, menacing. The audience should sense he is threatening even before Bret realizes it.

Sandy Barker: Mid to late 20's, pretty – has a sly, calculating, manner.

Bret Conway: 20's, attractive, intelligent, trusting and idealistic.

Mark Ryder: Late 20's to early 30's, trim and well-built, attractive, but not overly muscular. Bret's estranged lover. His anger can be explosive, but is only evident at key moments. At other times he can seem very appealing.

Eric Soames: Mid 20's to early 30's, trim, unconventionally attractive. Self-possessed and charismatic.

Police Detective Russell Craig: Mid-30's to early 40's, quirky in appearance, but not unattractive – a bit worn-looking. There is at once a burnt-out and an intense quality about him.

Gillian Hastings: 20's, strikingly good-looking, stylishly flamboyant – considers seduction a game meant to be played with many men. Gillian is pronounced with a hard "G".

(See Author Notes)

TIME AND PLACE:

1980's, in an upstate New York college town.

THE SET

The set, the main room of a studio apartment, is located on the second floor of an old Victorian house that is now an apartment house.

This apartment is entered from a hallway DR, and there is an emergency entry/exit - fire escape windows, a deck, and stairs UL - near the upstage corner of the room. During the performance, a full-length wall-mirror, upstage center, just stage right of the room's upstage corner, and near the fire escape exit, is revealed to be a third doorway into the apartment. It is also discovered that this is a see-through mirror, enabling the landlord Harold to spy unseen on his tenants.

An interior passageway UR leads to the studio apartment's kitchenette, dressing area, and bathroom - these spaces not visible to the audience. Between the DR hallway entrance, and the UR kitchenette/bathroom passageway, is a door leading to a small closet.

At stage left, there is a bay alcove with three double-hung windows with multiple small panes, and sheer curtains. They are the original windows. But the upstage fire escape windows are modern. Two window frames are hinged vertically so that when both are swung open a person can readily pass to or from the fire escape landing and steps. These windows also contain multiple small panes.

Upstage, behind the couch, and extending wall to wall, there is a step up to a raised floor (see plan view). This higher floor area accommodates the desk, and leads to the wall-mirror, and the fire escape/entrance.

The studio apartment is furnished with an eclectic mixture of used furniture, ranging in style from assembly-line period to contemporary. A downstage couch folds out into a double bed. Near the couch are a stuffed chair, a side table, and a table lamp. A study desk with a lamp, phone book and phone, and a chair are UR, and there is a chest of drawers between the stage right closet door and passageway. During Sandy's occupancy, there is also a small radio on the side table, and a computer on the desk. After Bret moves in, her easel, stool, and painting supply table are near the three double-hung windows in the alcove. An answering machine/phone is on the desk.

After Bret moves in, some of her sketches and paintings are displayed on the walls. What is most distinctive about them are the eyes, which are haunting and that some of the subject matter is threatening in nature.

SYNOPSIS OF SCENES

Act One, Scene One: 10 p.m. on a Friday in late September.

Act One, Scene Two: A weekday afternoon in late October.

Act One, Scene Three: Late in the afternoon, a few days later.

Act One, Scene Four: Later the same evening.

Act Two, Scene One: Later that night.

Act Two, Scene Two: Around nine the next evening.

Act Two, Scene Three: Two hours later.

SCENE CHANGES

It is suggested that eerie music be played during scene breaks.

COSTUMING NOTES

Harold: Drab beige or olive button-down shirts, and baggy cotton pants, with running shoes. His sleeves are always buttoned; his shirt is buttoned almost to the top.

Sandy: Simple, yet stylish clothing.

Bret: Jeans, and shirts and sweaters that complement her coloring and shape, but which are not flashy or tight. Stylish shoes or boots.

Mark: Not-too-faded jeans, and tasteful sweaters, tweed jackets, dark suede shoes.

Eric: Black jeans, black shirt and black running shoes. At times, a black leather jacket.

Craig: A plainclothesman. Dark slacks and a suit coat – professional enough, but not too stylish. Wrinkled white shirts, plain tie, a lined knee-length, dark raincoat, and dark leather shoes and gloves.

Gillian: Brightly colored, but not garish, tight clothing which emphasizes her shape.

Figure: Oversize outerwear, dark pants, and dark running shoes, with either a large, overhanging hood or a black ski mask *(see AUTHOR NOTES)*.

AUTHOR NOTES:

THE FIGURE at the end of I-1 and I-4 is MARK. However, this should never be apparent to the audience.

The FIGURE at the end of II-1 is CRAIG. However, this should never be apparent to the audience.

In each instance, the FIGURE'S identity is disguised by dark clothing and by the darkness of the room. MARK'S face is further hidden by a black ski mask. CRAIG'S face is hidden beneath the hood of a hooded sweatshirt.

In MARK'S case, it should be impossible to tell whether he has entered through the fire escape window or the mirror door. If lighting or staging constraints make this ambiguity impossible, he should always enter through the fire escape window.

THE NIGHTGOWN which is torn with the palette knife in II-2 can be set up ahead of time in the break between II-1 and II-2. A torn nightgown can be substituted so that the actor playing HAROLD does not actually have to destroy a nightgown during each performance, but it just appears as if he is stabbing it with the palette knife.

GILLIAN is pronounced with a hard "G".

CASCADILLA is pronounced: Cask - ah - dill - ah.

Also by the authors

Plays
Killing Dante

Poetry
At the Han-ku Pass

Non-Fiction
Writing the Award-Winning Play
Essay Writing Made Easy

ACT ONE -- SCENE ONE

At rise, the town clock SOUNDS *the first of ten chimes. In an upstate New York college town, it is 10 p.m. on a Friday in late September. Sandy Barker's apartment is nearly dark, its only* LIGHT *deriving from electrical lighting outdoors, filtering through the drawn alcove window curtains.*

(Having unlocked the DR *apartment door with his passkey,* **HAROLD** *enters and closes the door. He appears to be a mysterious figure, using his flashlight to find his way around the room. Crossing to the bed, he turns the bedside light on and turns off his flashlight)*

> The LIGHT *illuminates an abundance of college student clutter. The convertible couch is open; it is an unmade bed. There is a small, bright red suitcase next to the apartment door* DR.

> **HAROLD** *is dressed in baggy khakis, running shoes, and a beige, long-sleeved shirt with his collar unbuttoned. Around his waist is a tool belt with a hammer, screwdriver, and tape measure.*

*(***HAROLD** *is carrying a gift-wrapped package with a large red bow. He is uncertain as to where to put the package, trying first the top of the chest of drawers, and then the side table near the bed, before carefully placing it on the bed.*

(But, irresistibly drawn to it, he again picks up the package, contemplating opening it. Finally, as if resisting an overpowering urge, he throws the package back on the bed and quickly crosses to the dresser UR. *Without hesitation he opens the top drawer and pulls out a pair of women's underpants. He stares at them as if fixated)*

> SOUNDS and **SANDY BARKER** *humming, off, outside the* DR *door are heard.*

(Cramming the underpants back into the drawer and closing the drawer, **HAROLD** *then backs against the wall mirror upstage, where he freezes, watching intently.*

*(***SANDY** *enters the apartment, carrying her purse. Surprised and alarmed to find the table lamp on, she immediately turns on the overhead light and scans the room)*

SANDY

Who's here?

> **SANDY** *is dressed casually and tastefully as would befit a graduate student.*

HAROLD

It's only me, Miss Barker.

SANDY
(Seeing HAROLD, SHE *is at once relieved)*
Mr. Lemb! You scared the hell out of me!
*(*SHE *places her purse on the desk and turns on the desk lamp)*
A dim LIGHT *emanates from the lamp.*

HAROLD
Sorry. I didn't intend to frighten you.
SANDY
You weren't spying on me, were you?
HAROLD
Of course not!
(Holding up a tape measure.)
I was just measuring that broken window you asked me to fix.
SANDY
(Taking off HER *jacket)*
Glad you're finally getting around to it. You've seen the Cayuga Press about that rapist on the loose, haven't you? Anyone could come right up that fire escape and through the windows.

HAROLD
I don't follow the news.
SANDY
Well, he's attacked three women in the past three months. Attacked them in their apartments.
HAROLD
But certainly any rapist would know there's a man living here.
SANDY
A man? You're referring to yourself? No offense, but I'd rather have the window fixed.
HAROLD
Well, maybe I would have fixed it sooner if you'd paid your rent on time.
SANDY
(Searching in HER *purse, she pulls out a rent check and hands it to* HIM)*
I almost forgot about you. I didn't think you'd mind. Here it is.
HAROLD
I just want the rent paid on time. That's all.
Loud BANGING *is heard, originating off,* DR.
SANDY
There he goes again. What's he doing in there, anyhow?

HAROLD

I never discuss my tenants' private lives, Miss Barker, even if I knew what they were.

SANDY

Of course not. Who would you discuss them with?

HAROLD

If the noise bothers you, I could speak to him.

SANDY

No, don't worry about it. Once I'm asleep, I sleep like the dead.

(SHE *picks up the package*)

What's this? Not a present from you, Mr. Lemb?

HAROLD

Someone left it on your doorstep. I just brought it in for you.

SANDY

Relax. I must have a secret admirer.

(SHE *silently reads the attached card, then opens the package and pulls out a black floor-length nightgown with thin straps and a plunging neckline. She holds it against her body*)

Why, you're blushing, Mr. Lemb.

HAROLD

Excuse me. I have work to do.

SANDY

I'm leaving first thing in the morning and won't be back until Sunday night. That should give you plenty of time to fix that window.

HAROLD

I'll go out for the glass tomorrow. All right?

SANDY

Well, I know how infrequently you get out.

HAROLD

How do you know?

SANDY

You practically live like a mole down there. If your name weren't on the mailbox, I'd hardly know you live right below me.

HAROLD

There's no need for you to see me, is there? Except when I collect the rent check and do the repairs. Goodnight.

(**HAROLD** *exits* DR. **SANDY** *closes and locks the door. She turns on the radio and a small bedside lamp*)

Soft rock MUSIC *is heard.*

(*SANDY carries the nightgown upstage to the full-length wall mirror, where she holds the nightgown before her approvingly*)

SANDY

I knew you couldn't stay away.

(*She then crosses to the desk and phones. After a moment, she looks at her watch.*

(*Angrily*)

Where are you?

(*SHE hangs up, turns off the overhead light, then exits with the nightgown through the dressing area door at stage right*)

> LIGHT *from the dressing area is cast against part of the* UL *wall so that we can see the silhouette of* **SANDY** *as she changes into the nightgown. The silhouette is erotic and seductive.*
> The LIGHT *in the dressing area is turned* OFF.

(*SANDY reënters, wearing the nightgown.* SHE *dances upstage to the full-length mirror, where she models the nightgown*)

> *There is* KNOCKING *at the apartment door,* DR.

You *were* on your way!

(*Expecting her lover,* **SANDY** *rushes to the apartment door,* DR, *and flings it open -- to reveal* **BRET CONWAY**)

> **BRET** *is dressed casually in jeans and a sweater over a buttoned-down shirt and a lightweight jacket.*

Bret! This is a surprise!

BRET

I was just walking by and saw your light on. Thought I'd come up.

(*SHE enters and stands just inside the door*)

But it looks like you're about ready for bed.

SANDY

(*Impatiently, with no intention of making* **BRET** *feel welcome*)

I have to get up early tomorrow. I'm going away for the weekend.

BRET

What a coincidence. So is Mark.

SANDY

Well, I hope your boyfriend has fun. Especially since he's left me with a stack of graduate papers to grade.

(*SHE yawns, then starts to usher* **BRET** *out*)

I appreciate the visit, but it is late . . .

BRET

The truth is, I didn't just happen to see your lights on. I've got to talk to someone and I thought of you.

SANDY

I suppose I should be flattered. It's not as though you and I are good friends.

BRET

It's about Mark.

SANDY

What about Mark?

BRET

I think he's having an affair with someone.

SANDY

Well, then -- come in.

(*SANDY* stands back. *BRET* enters the room and looks about. *SANDY* turns on the overhead light and then crosses to the radio and turns it off)

    The MUSIC *ceases.*

Did Mark tell you he's having an affair?

BRET

I accused him just before he left for that conference in Syracuse. He denied it. Proved his point by breaking the chairs. But I'm not stupid. There are all the signs. The mysterious phone calls. The late nights. The lame excuses.

SANDY

Do you have any idea who the other woman is?

BRET

I have my suspicions. Someone he met through the university.

SANDY

Do you think Mark's stupid enough to go after one of his young students? If that got out, he'd lose any chance at tenure, maybe even his precious career.

BRET

It's not one of his students. I thought you might know who it is.

SANDY

I'm not Mark's confessor -- only his graduate assistant.

BRET

And his friend.

SANDY

Of course.

BRET

Are you more than friends? Are you the one involved with Mark?

SANDY

Oh, really, Bret! I don't know whether to be offended or amused.

BRET

That's not an answer.

SANDY

Of course I'm involved with Mark – I grade his students' boring papers, work endlessly on that damn book he hopes will get him tenure. He doesn't realize how dependent he is on me. But as for Mark's private life, I'm afraid I can't help you.

BRET

Are you saying it's not you?

SANDY

Look at you, poor thing. I don't know who Mark's having an affair with. But even if I did, wouldn't my telling you be betraying Mark's trust in me? Mark always said you valued trust.

BRET

I do.

SANDY

Well, you can appreciate the bind I'd be in – if I did know something. But maybe you should realize there's a side of Mark you don't know.

BRET

What do you mean?

SANDY

Maybe this other woman fulfills some need in him that you can't – or won't.

BRET

Do you think a relationship is that simple? That it depends on what one will or will not do in the dark?

SANDY

Sometimes it is that simple.

BRET

I have these fantasies about letting her have it.

SANDY

Really? That's so unlike you, Bret.

BRET

And what am I usually like? Naïve? Gullible?

(There is a silence between THEM*)*

Well, it doesn't matter. I think he's going to end it.

SANDY

With you?

BRET

No. With her.

SANDY

Why do you think that?

BRET

Because, despite everything, I know Mark loves me. He and I were talking about getting married.

SANDY

Before he started seeing someone else, I would imagine.

(With increased impatience)

Well, I guess I haven't been much help to you.

BRET

No. You've been very helpful. Thank you for listening to me, especially since it's so late — you must still have to pack.

SANDY

I already have packed.

(**SANDY** *indicates the suitcase near the* DR *door, as she holds the door open for* BRET. BRET *crosses to the door, then pauses)*

BRET

You were right about one thing.

SANDY

What's that?

BRET

There is a side to Mark that's not very appealing. But I suppose that's true of everyone.

SANDY

Perhaps you should choose your friends more carefully. Goodnight, Bret.

BRET

Goodnight, Sandy.

(SHE exits.

(**SANDY** *closes the apartment door behind* BRET. She *crosses to the desk and punches in a number on the telephone. She impatiently waits for an answer, but after receiving none, she hangs up angrily)*

SANDY

(Angrily)

Well, I guess you're not coming after all.

(SHE crosses to the DR apartment door and turns off the overhead light then crosses to the radio and turns it on)

> *The room is only dimly LIT by the desk and bedside lamps.*
> *There is the SOUND of soft, moody MUSIC.*

(SANDY crosses to the bed, gets in, turns off the bedside lamp and settles down on the bed to sleep)

> *LIGHT -- so dim as to cause the room's furnishings to appear in barely discernible shadow -- emanates from the electrical LIGHT from outdoors filtering through the drawn alcove window curtains and from the desk lamp.*

(A FIGURE enters, emerging from the shadows from the upstage corner of the room where both the full-length mirror and the fire escape windows are located. It is impossible to tell the precise point of entry. The face is obscured by a black ski mask and wears dark clothing

(The FIGURE moves stealthily, almost ghost-like, downstage until it halts behind the bed. The FIGURE looks down at the reclining **SANDY** *who is unaware of the presence)*

> FADE to BLACK
> END *of* SCENE ONE

(There is a minimal interval between scenes. Eerie music should be played between scenes)

ACT ONE -- SCENE TWO

> *A weekday afternoon in late October. The apartment is devoid of any personal items. The bed is folded into a couch. The fire escape windows are wide open, as is the hallway door DR. The curtains are open.*

(HAROLD is dusting the room)

> **HAROLD** *is dressed in baggy khakis, running shoes, and a beige, long-sleeved shirt buttoned at the sleeves.*

(HE looks about, pleased with his work, then exits into the kitchenette/dressing area at UR. Hesitantly, BRET appears at the open hallway door DR)

> *SHE is dressed in jeans, leather boots, a pullover sweater, and a parka and carries a shoulder bag.*

> **BRET**

(Knocking on the open door)

Hello?

(**HAROLD** *peeks out of the kitchenette/dressing room doorway* UR, *silently watching. Hearing no reply,* **BRET** *enters*)
Anyone here?
(SHE *looks around the room, then crosses to the alcove windows, and scans the vista*)

HAROLD
(Fully reëntering, and crossing to the mirror)
The view from here is captivating.

BRET
(Turning, startled)
Oh! I didn't know anyone was here.

HAROLD
(Reciting as if reading from an ad)
"Bright, roomy second-floor studio."

BRET
Excuse me?

HAROLD
"Neat single University student, non-smoker preferred. No dogs. Reasonable rent for the right person." That's what the ad said.

BRET
The ad?

HAROLD
I'm **HAROLD** Lemb, the landlord. You're here because of the ad, aren't you?

BRET
Actually I'm here because of Sandy Barker. I'm -- a friend of hers.

HAROLD
Then you must know what happened.

BRET
I know what the police say – she left town a month ago and never came back.

HAROLD
She broke the lease. Left me trying to find a suitable tenant to replace her. That's what happened. Not to mention the police. They don't have any respect for a person's privacy.

BRET
(Walking around the room)
Then you don't know why she left?

HAROLD

I assumed she dropped out. College students are never very reliable. All that matters to me is I've got this place to rent. It isn't easy, you know -- finding the right person.

(**HAROLD** *is watching* **BRET** *intently*)

BRET

No, it isn't easy. Just when you think you've found the right person, they disappoint you. . . . So you have no idea what happened to her?

HAROLD

Maybe nothing happened to her. People disappear every day for their own reasons. She could have gotten on a bus -- gone anywhere.

BRET

That's what the police think.

HAROLD

Well, that should settle it.

BRET

(Crossing to the wall mirror)

But I wonder -- do you remember any of Sandy's -- visitors? Anyone who came here often?

HAROLD

I'm not in the habit of spying on my tenants.

BRET

I didn't mean to suggest that.

(Touching the mirror frame)

What a beautiful mirror. Is it an antique?

HAROLD

No. I made it.

BRET

Why, how talented you are, Mr. Lemb. It's so large. You can see the whole apartment in it.

(**MARK**, *having quietly entered the hallway from downstairs, appears in the open doorway DR, where he stands, listening to what is being said. The* OTHERS *do not see him*)

> **MARK** *is tall and good-looking, and is dressed in jeans, running shoes, a pullover sweater, and a jacket.*

HAROLD

Yes, if you stand in just the right spot . . .

(**HAROLD** *points toward the passageway UR*)

The bathroom and kitchenette are through here. This couch folds into a bed. Maybe *you're* looking for a place? Reasonable rent for the right person.

BRET

Me? . . . I just thought you might have noticed someone that last night Sandy was here.

MARK

(Crossing into the apartment)

What the hell's going on here?

BRET

Mark!

HAROLD

(Startled -- to **BRET***)*

What's he doing here?

MARK

Who the hell are you?

BRET

This is the landlord, Mark.

HAROLD

I don't want any trouble.

BRET

There won't be any trouble.

MARK

Bret, what are you doing here?

BRET

Why shouldn't I be *here*? Why are *you* here?

MARK

I followed you. I've been worried about you.

BRET

I have to know about Sandy.

MARK

For God's sake, Bret! Not that again! Look around you, Bret. Sandy doesn't live here anymore. You won't find any answers about her here.

BRET

But you know the answers, don't you? You two had been working so closely together. You'd obviously gotten to know her *quite* well.

MARK

It was those damn hang-up calls that got you started on all this, wasn't it? Well, they've stopped, haven't they?

BRET

(Pointedly)

Yes. They stopped -- just about the same time Sandy left town.

MARK

Look -- Sandy's probably in Aspen with some guy. Remember that ski bum she ran off with last year, over Christmas?

BRET

Yes, I remember.

MARK

She didn't tell anyone where she was going *that* time, did she?

BRET

And you haven't spoken to her this whole time? Haven't seen her?

MARK

I wish to hell I had. Who do you think has been stuck with grading all my students' papers since she left? Yours truly. Not to mention getting my book finished. Now come on. Let's forget about Sandy and go home.

BRET

I don't want to go home.

MARK

What?

BRET

I'm not sure I believe you, Mark.

MARK

What more do you want? What else do I have to say to convince you?

BRET

Ever since you trashed our apartment – I'm not sure I know who you are anymore.

MARK

So I broke a few chairs. Jesus, that was over a month ago! Will you listen to me? There is no one else! I only want you! Damn it, Bret! Everything I've done, I've done for you!

BRET

For me?!

MARK

For us! Can't you understand that?

BRET

You haven't done anything for me. The job at this college – your career -- everything you've done was for yourself.

MARK

You have no idea what I've done for you.

(**MARK** *grabs* **BRET**'S *arms and pulls her to him*)

Why don't you want what I want anymore?

(**HAROLD** *backs away from them until he is against the wall mirror. He watches intently*)

BRET

(Trying to break away)

Mark, let me go!

MARK

Are you coming home with me or not?

BRET

No! No, I'm not! I've just decided! I'm leaving! I'm moving out!

MARK

(Holding HER *more tightly)*

Moving out? You can't!

(When **MARK** *does not loosen his grasp,* **BRET** *furiously frees a hand and slaps him across the face.*

(Remorsefully)

I'm sorry, Bret.

BRET

Get out!

MARK

Bret -- Please --

BRET

Just get out!

(**MARK** *exits* DR)

HAROLD

Did he hurt you?

BRET

I'm afraid we hurt each other. . . . I'm sorry about that scene, Mr. Lemb.

HAROLD

Is that your boyfriend?

BRET

Was my boyfriend. He never used to be like that.

(SHE hesitates)

I don't know what I'll do now. I can't go home . . .

HAROLD

This apartment is available. If you're interested.

BRET

This apartment?

HAROLD

You won't find much else out there this late in the year. Unless you don't mind holes in the walls and rats. Take a look at the kitchenette and the bathroom. There's also a dressing area.

*(As **BRET** exits into the stage right passageway, **HAROLD** watches her with interest)*

There have been some interested parties, but, as you can see, it's a special place.

BRET

(Reëntering)

It would be perfect, if you really mean it.

HAROLD

I can't let just anyone have it. . . . People can be so careless and brutal sometimes.

BRET

I'm not like that.

HAROLD

Oh, I can see that you're not like other people at all.

BRET

Does this mean that I can have the apartment?

HAROLD

I prefer that no one but the tenant spends the night.

BRET

I understand.

HAROLD

I don't want any trouble. Especially from that — friend of yours.

BRET

Believe me. I just want to be by myself for awhile.

HAROLD

I've been waiting for the right person. It's yours, if you want it.

BRET

Oh, thank you, Mr. Lemb. You're a godsend. When could I move it?

HAROLD

The sooner the better. The place is empty now, just waiting for you. If you'll follow me downstairs, I have a standard lease in my apartment. You see, I'll be right below you. A young woman all alone, such as yourself, should feel secure knowing there's a man like me around.

(THEY *exit* DR)

BLACKOUT.

END *of* SCENE TWO

[There is a minimal interval between scenes. Eerie music should be played between scenes]

ACT ONE -- SCENE THREE

It is late in the afternoon, a few days later.

The glow of a sunset brightens the windows. As the scene progresses, the lighting DIMS indicating falling darkness.

The apartment is filled with Bret's possessions. Some of Bret's charcoal drawings are taped to the walls. They are realistic representations. The eyes, which are haunting, are their most distinctive feature. Some of the drawings contain threatening subject matter. The convertible couch is closed, and the hallway door DR is closed.

(**BRET** *is on a stool, painting on a canvas on a large easel positioned to catch the light from the alcove windows)*

The painting is turned away from the audience. On a small stand next to the easel, there are a large glass jar containing a few paintbrushes, a smaller jar a quarter full of linseed oil, a paint-stained rag, and a palette knife. Next to the stand is a can of turpentine.

SHE is wearing a painting shirt over another shirt, and jeans.

A loud BANGING is heard off, DR.

(**BRET** *looks from her work toward the direction of the noise)*

The BANGING stops.

(**BRET** *goes back to her work for a moment, then looks around uneasily, as if she senses someone is in the room with her)*

BRET

Is someone here?

(SHE *crosses to the lamp next to the couch, and turns it on)*

> *The lamp* LIGHTS, *initially having little effect on the late afternoon room lighting.*
> *(Checking,* **BRET** *crosses in front of the mirror and glances into the area leading to the offstage kitchenette/dressing area* UR, *then crosses quickly to the light switch* DR, *and turns on the overhead light)*
> *The room* BRIGHTENS.
> *(Still unsettled, trying to shake off the feeling.)*

Why is it always so damned hot in here? *That* I'm not imagining.

> *(SHE takes off her painting shirt, trying to cool herself off, to no avail. Then she crosses to one of the bay alcove windows and attempts to open it, but it is stuck. She tries the other two, but they, also, are stuck)*
> *A loud* BANGING, *then a* SCRAPING, *is heard off,* DR.

God! What *is* that noise?

*(***BRET*** crosses to the DR door and opens it. She is startled to find* **HAROLD** *standing at the doorway, giving every evidence of having been eavesdropping. He is carrying a package like the one in I-1)*

Mr. Lemb!

HAROLD
(Quickly handing HER *the package)*
This is for you. It was left outside your door.

BRET
(Taking the package)
Outside my door? Who left it?

HAROLD
I didn't see. There's a card.

BRET
(Examining the card, then reading aloud)
"For the woman of my dreams" . . .

> *(***BRET*** contemplates opening the package, but finally crosses to the dresser and puts the package on top.* **HAROLD** *makes a move to leave)*

Mr. Lemb, if you have a minute, could you unstick one of those windows? I don't know about your apartment downstairs, but it's always so hot in mine.

HAROLD
I'll help you any way I can.
(HE crosses to the alcove windows, and struggles to open them)
They're painted shut, I'm afraid.

BRET
Painted shut? . . . It makes me feel a bit claustrophobic, not being

able to open the windows.

HAROLD

These fire escape windows open.

BRET

I wouldn't feel safe leaving them open. I'm sure you've heard about that rapist. Which reminds me, the pane near the window lock is missing.   Could you fix that when you fix the other windows?

HAROLD

I'll have to measure that pane. I'll come back later and take care of everything.

BRET

I appreciate it.

(Glancing out one of the windows, suddenly concerned)

Strange   . . .   that man's still there.   The one who's always watching this house.

HAROLD

(Also disturbed, crossing to the window)

What man? What do you mean, watching this house?

BRET

See him down there by the street light?

HAROLD

Where?

BRET

There! He's walking away -- up the street. He's the same man I've seen every day since I moved in. Always looking up at these windows.

HAROLD

It's you he's watching.

BRET

Me?

HAROLD

I knew I was taking a chance letting you in. I knew he was trouble. Always prowling around. Bothering Miss Barker late at night.

BRET

You've seen that man before? When Sandy lived here?

HAROLD

Not that man. The one with the temper. Your boyfriend. He was always here.

BRET

What do you mean he was always here?

HAROLD

I've already told the police. Now I just want to be left alone.

(Crossing quickly to the door, DR*)*

I'll come back to measure that pane.

(As **HAROLD** *exits* DR, *he bumps into* **GILLIAN HASTINGS***, who is entering into the room)*

> **GILL** *is sexy and striking, dressed as a fashionable, sophisticated college student would dress.*

BRET

Gillian!

GILL

Bret, Sweetie!

*(*THEY *hug warmly)*

BRET

God, I'm glad to see you!

GILL

I missed you, too.

(Surveying the apartment)

Your usual interesting decor, I see -- tormented artist meets Goodwill.

BRET

What are you doing here?

GILL

I could ask you the same question.

BRET

But you're supposed to be in Paris -- becoming as one with the natives.

GILL

(Removing HER *coat)*

Oh, I became one with them, all right. Did you know that most European men aren't circumcised?

BRET

Gill! You're too much!

GILL

That's what they all said. How Father ever found out, I'll never know.

BRET

What happened?

GILL

He laid down the law, with his usual finesse, and the usual cutting off my allowance. He said something about having sent me to Europe to study art, not the artists. . . . God, it's hot in here.

(*SHE crosses to the alcove windows, trying unsuccessfully to open one*)

BRET

Don't bother. They're stuck.

GILL

Stuck! Just like I feel.   . . .   Sweetie, how about some cappuccino? I'm desperate for a pick-me-up.

BRET

Sorry. I only have instant coffee.

GILL

Instant? How painfully American. It's so depressing to be back. But I have a solution for that. Voilà!

(*SHE reaches into her handbag for a bottle of wine and a corkscrew*)

A little gift for a little toast. All we need are glasses.

BRET

That I have.

(*While **BRET** quickly exits through the dressing/kitchen door, UR, and returns with two glasses, **GILL** opens the bottle, then pours the wine*)

Are you staying at Alec's?

GILL

I needed some place to put my luggage. Oh, don't get me wrong. Alec has his . . . charms. Or -- at least there's one I can think of. But it's hardly love ever after.

(*Raising HER glass to toast*)

Salut!

BRET

Salut!

(*THEY toast and drink*)

GILL

Speaking of love ever after -- what *are* you doing here? What about Mark?

BRET

It's over, Gill. That's all.

GILL

Over? I can't believe it. I thought you two were going to tie the knot.

BRET

Not exactly.   Mark and I haven't made love in almost two months.

GILL

Two months! My God! Then who are you sleeping with?

BRET

No one, Gill.

GILL

No one? How awful!

BRET

Mark keeps trying to pressure me, but I just haven't been able to feel comfortable with him — not since I accused him of sleeping with Sandy.

GILL

Sandy? Are you sure?

BRET

They both denied it.

GILL

But you don't believe them. And you can't forgive him, is that it?

BRET

Forgive him? How can I forgive something he still won't admit?

GILL

Everyone makes mistakes, Bret. Besides, whatever he had with Sandy must have ended. Alec told me she left school.

BRET

No one's heard from her. No one knows where she is. Not even Mark -- or so he says.

GILL

You know Sandy. It's quite like her -- leaving town without a word to anyone.

BRET

Before I moved in here, I would have agreed with you. But now--

GILL

Now what?

BRET

I don't know. It's just that — I have this strange feeling — as if someone's been watching me.

GILL

Watching you?

BRET

Do you feel it? It's almost as if . . . someone else is in here. In this room . . . watching us now.

GILL

It's those paintings of yours. You've always had a touch of the morbid, you know. As usual, your imagination is working overtime.

BRET

(Looking out of an alcove window)

No – I've seen a man out there -- watching this house

        A *loud* BANGING *is heard off,* DR.

GILL

What the hell is that?

BRET

I think it's my neighbor. He bangs away all night.

GILL

Sounds promising.

BRET

Oh, Gill, I'm so glad you're back.

GILL

Don't worry. Everything will turn out all right. You'll see.

BRET

I hope you're right.

GILL

(Putting on HER *coat, then crossing to the* DR *apartment door)*

Well, I hate to say it, but I must be off. I have to meet Alec and I'm late already. I just wanted you to know I'm back -- and I'm thinking of you.

BRET

Thanks, Gill. It's great knowing you're here. Don't forget to call me. Soon.

GILL

When I get settled. Ciao, baby.

*(*GILL *blows a kiss and exits* DR, *not fully closing the door. The same red suitcase as in I-I is in the hallway.*

*(*BRET *crosses to the dresser and picks up the package. She opens it and pulls out a full-length black nightgown similar to the one Sandy received. After several beats,* ERIC *appears in the doorway* DR. *He is holding a hammer in a way that seems menacing. A chisel protrudes from his back pocket. He crosses a few steps into the room)*

ERIC *is dressed in black jeans, a black sweatshirt, and black sneakers.*

(**BRET** *turns, startled at the sight of* **ERIC**. *When she sees that he is carrying a hammer, she is frightened and drops the nightgown)*

BRET

Who . . . who are you?

ERIC

Excuse me. I didn't mean to frighten you.

BRET

What do you want?

ERIC

I'm sorry. I did frighten you. I'm your neighbor from across the hall.

BRET

(Less frightened, but still wary)

My neighbor?

ERIC

Eric Soames. And you're Bret Conway. I noticed you when you first moved in.

BRET

Did you really?

ERIC

Harold said you needed some help opening your windows.

(Holding up HIS *tools)*

May I?

BRET

Well – yes. They all seem to be stuck. And it gets so hot in here.

ERIC

It's these old places. They're either broiling or stone cold.

*(*HE *crosses to the alcove windows and begins working on them)*

BRET

Thanks.

ERIC

No problem. I do this sort of thing for a living.

BRET

You open windows for a living?

ERIC

I do carpenter work around Collegetown to pay the bills. I picked up the trade traveling around the country for a few years -- trying to find myself, as they say.

BRET
Any luck?

ERIC
Let's just say I ended up broke in a redneck dust bowl of a town in west Texas. But at least by then I had discovered my true ambition.

BRET
Which is . . . ?

ERIC
To be an artist – a struggling one at the moment.

BRET
We have something in common – I'm a painter. Struggling, as well.

ERIC
I create constructions. I hope all my hammering hasn't been bothering you.

BRET
So that explains the strange noises I've been hearing. Just what kind of constructions are you building in there?

ERIC
I'm afraid it's a superstition of mine not to discuss my work until it's finished.

BRET
You can trust me -- being a fellow struggling artist, I'd understand.

ERIC
(After viewing HER *painting for a brief moment)*
You just might. . . . I get my materials from other people's garbage.

BRET
Garbage?

ERIC
You'd be surprised what people throw away. Wrought iron, wood, glass. I take whatever strikes my interest.

BRET
Nothing decaying -- I hope.

ERIC
My work is hard to describe. You'd have to see it.

BRET
I'd like to.

ERIC

Perhaps when my next sculpture is finished, I'll give you a private showing.

(Having managed to open the window only partially)

BRET

That's fine. I just need a bit of air. Thanks. Maybe the landlord would pay you to fix that broken fire escape window.

ERIC

(Moving on to work at the next window)

Harold's pretty handy on his own. He doesn't like other people poking around his house.

BRET

Why? What's he hiding?

ERIC

Who knows? Maybe himself. Haven't you noticed how he creeps around?

BRET

Well, yes. But he seems so harmless. You make him sound a little scary.

ERIC

I've upset you. Really -- I wouldn't worry. I can hardly imagine him doing anything other than look at you.

*(**ERIC** has managed to open the second window partially)*

BRET

Sometimes I feel like someone's been in here. It's as if – I don't know – as if they've left behind their presence – kind of like a scent. Do you think it could be Harold?

ERIC

Believe me, he wouldn't do anything to scare you away from this apartment. He's so particular about whom he rents to. He prefers pretty, young women, you know.

BRET

So what about you?

ERIC

I prefer pretty, young women, too. . . . I guess Harold rented to me because I can be so persuasive. . . . But I really wouldn't worry about him. I think he's actually afraid of us. We're the cats, you see. He watches us so we won't pounce on *him*.

BRET

Are you sure?

ERIC

I can usually tell what a person is like. You, for instance, are very attractive, sensitive, intelligent. And you're trusting.

BRET

I'm not sure I am, anymore.

ERIC

Yes, you are. Perhaps too trusting. You let me into your apartment without question.

BRET

I don't remember you asking permission.

ERIC

And there's a dark side to you — something you're hiding.

BRET

How can you determine that, Sherlock?

ERIC

(HE *studies the painting on the easel)*

Your painting -- it has a certain edge -- a sense of danger -- real potential. Needs work, of course.

BRET

You're lucky I don't mind people looking at my work. Some people I've met aren't so trusting.

ERIC

I have a sort of sixth sense for what people will allow.

BRET

Can you read me so easily?

ERIC

The woman is naked, her back turned. We can't see her face. She is very tense -- perhaps afraid. She half turns to a figure just emerging from the shadows, both faces -- hidden from us. The feeling is ominous, but strangely exciting. He's going to attack her . . . or are they about to have sex? Have you always thought of sex as being so terrifying?

BRET

I'm not sure I'm ready for the psychoanalysis, Dr. Soames.

ERIC

We all have shadows, secrets we don't want to admit to others. . . . If you drew me, do you think you'd find mine?

BRET

You're trickier than most. Most people's eyes give them away. But yours don't want to give up too much.

ERIC

Maybe I don't trust you enough.

BRET

There's no reason not to trust me.

ERIC

I'd have to get to know you better before deciding that.

BRET

Is that why you don't want anyone to see what you're working on? You don't trust anyone enough?

ERIC

There's a flow to my work that can't be interrupted. What I create my way is solely my own. Like you, I don't see the point in being analyzed.

BRET

You don't want to risk exposure, is that it?

ERIC

I take my own risks. Let's just say I like to remain in control. . . . Maybe we could go out for a drink sometime, and explore just exactly what I *am* willing to give up.

BRET

Maybe.

ERIC

You're right about someone's scent taking over a place. Yours has already filled this room.

BRET

And what scent is that?

ERIC

(HE *picks up the jar of turpentine on the stand, and then puts it down)*

The aroma of turpentine and oil.

BRET

Not very alluring, I'm afraid.

ERIC

On the contrary.

(HE *slowly runs a finger along* HER *cheek, then holds it up for her to see)*

I like that. A smear of paint, like a battle scar -- it betrays you.

BRET

(Moving away from HIS *touch)*

Thanks for opening the windows.

ERIC
Anytime you need me -- I'm right next door.
BRET
I'll keep that in mind.
ERIC
(Crossing to DR door, seeing the red suitcase, then carrying it into the room)
Oh, by the way, you left your suitcase in the hall.
BRET
That's not mine.
ERIC
(Examining the suitcase's ID tag)
It has this address on it.
BRET
My God, I think it's Sandy's.
*(**BRET** opens it)*
This *is* the suitcase Sandy left town with. How did it get in the hall?
*(**MARK** appears at the open apartment doorway, DR. Silently, he listens)*

> **MARK** *is dressed in dark slacks, a maroon sweater and black shoes, and wears a tweed jacket.*

ERIC
Maybe someone found it somewhere, and just returned it.
MARK
(Abruptly entering DR)
Am I interrupting something?
BRET
(Startled)
Mark! I wasn't expecting you.
MARK
So I see. Don't I rate an introduction?
(The MEN silently size up one another)
BRET
This is my neighbor, Eric Soames. He was just helping me with the windows.
MARK
How very neighborly.
BRET
This is my -- friend -- Mark Ryder.

MARK

I would say we were much more than friends, wouldn't you, Bret?

ERIC

Time to get back to other people's garbage. . . . Don't forget that drink sometime, Bret. And remember, I'm always across the hall, if Harold ever corners you in the pantry.

(With a disdainful glance at **MARK***,* **ERIC** *exits DR, closing the door)*

MARK

What did all of that mean?

BRET

It doesn't mean anything. But this does.

(Indicating Sandy's suitcase)

Someone left that in the hall.

MARK

So?

BRET

It's Sandy's.

MARK

What's it doing here?

BRET

Someone must have found it abandoned somewhere in Cayuga. Maybe Sandy didn't just leave on her own. Maybe – maybe something happened to her.

MARK

Just because that suitcase turns up? How do you know this is the same suitcase?

BRET

Because I saw it. I came here that night to see Sandy.

MARK

You were here?

BRET

It looked like she was expecting someone. Was it *you* Sandy was waiting for?

MARK

You know I was on my way to that conference in Syracuse. I checked in around eleven on Friday. You can call the hotel, if you want.

BRET

I know you came here to see Sandy many nights. Mr. Lemb saw

you. *Were* you her lover, Mark?

MARK

(After a pause)

The truth is -- I did spend a lot of time here with Sandy.

BRET

Oh, Mark!

MARK

It's not what you think.

BRET

Isn't it? Isn't it *exactly* what I think? That you've betrayed me! Lied to me! That you're lying still!

MARK

Sandy was nothing to me! I was here all those nights to work on my book.

BRET

Your book?

MARK

I suppose I could have forced her to work on my office computer until two in the morning. But she had a computer here, so we agreed whenever I had my revisions ready, I'd just bring them over.

BRET

Is that really all?

MARK

Yeah, that's all. Just the book. Just my whole God damn career down the tubes if I don't get the damn thing finished and published. Just everything I've worked for my whole life, that's all.

BRET

Why didn't you just tell me all this from the beginning?

MARK

Your reaction just now is precisely why I didn't tell you before. I knew you'd be suspicious – for no reason.

BRET

I don't know what to say.

MARK

Then don't say anything. Just listen.

(Pause, now imploring)

I came here to apologize for my behavior over the past month. . . . I've been under a lot of stress with Sandy leaving me in the lurch the way she did. Not that that excuses anything. I know I've been a complete idiot.

(Taking HER *hands and drawing her closer)*

Maybe this separation has been good for us. I know now -- you mean everything to me. I realize how much I miss you, how much I need you. I hope you've missed me.

BRET

(After a pause)

I *have* missed you.

MARK

All of the things we've shared -- not so easy to forget.

BRET

No -- not so easy to forget.

MARK

Do you remember that little inn we went to in Maine, last fall?

BRET

Yes. I remember waking up in the morning, looking out at the sea. We hiked everyday in the mountains until we were exhausted.

MARK

Not too exhausted. Remember the canopied bed and the fire in our bedroom at night? I remember you lying naked in the firelight. Wanting me -- the way I wanted you.

BRET

Oh! I did want you! I've never been happier, never felt freer.

MARK

I'll never forget how you looked, how you felt those nights, making love.

BRET

. . . and afterwards we left the windows open for the sea breeze . . .

MARK

. . . and made love again under our down comforter . . .

BRET

. . . listening to the sound of the sea. I remember. Those were such perfect days . . .

MARK

. . . and nights.

BRET

Yes. When I remember our best times -- we're at that little inn,

and it's fall, and we're lying together listening to the sound of the sea.
MARK
Bret, we could go back there on fall break.
BRET
If only we could . . .
MARK
We can. It's just what we need.
BRET
Can we go back, Mark? So much has happened.
MARK
Nothing has happened to change how I feel about you, **BRET**.
Believe me.
BRET
I want to believe you.
MARK
There's no one else for me, Bret.. There's only you. Will you at least think about going to the inn?

BRET
Yes, I'll think about it. I haven't given up on you yet, Mr. Ryder.
MARK
I promise you , Bret. I'll do anything to bring you back to me. . . . But for now, will you have dinner with me at the Hillside? I have just enough time before class.
BRET
OK. Let me just change my shirt.

(Crossing to the chest of drawers, SHE *selects a shirt.*

*(***CRAIG** *has appeared on the fire escape deck outside the upstage windows)*
It is DARK *outside, except for the faint outdoor* LIGHTING *which dimly illuminates the fire escape and* **CRAIG***.*
*(***CRAIG** *peers inside for a moment, then pulls back into the shadows)*
MARK
By the way, Gillian called for you at my place. I told her you lived here now.
BRET
(Now at the mirror, changing shirts)
She stopped by a little while ago. She's staying with that jerk she met last spring.

MARK

(Intently watching **BRET** *as she takes off her shirt and puts on a new one)*

You mean Larry?

BRET

Not that jerk, the other one.

(As SHE *turns to* **MARK**, *buttoning her shirt)*

Gill doesn't know what she wants.

MARK

(Approaching **BRET***)*

I do . . .

(Gently pulling **BRET** *toward* HIM, **MARK** *kisses her, and she responds)*

BRET

(Gently pulling away from HIM*)*

I guess you do. But I don't think I'm ready to try on your gift just yet.

MARK

What gift?

BRET

How quickly they forget.

(Picking up the nightgown and holding it in front of HER*)*

Now do you remember?

MARK

Where did you get that?

*(***CRAIG** *appears again outside the fire escape window)*

CRAIG *wears a dark gray raincoat over a dark, not-too-stylish suit, a white shirt, and a tie.*

BRET

(Dropping the nightgown)

Mark! There's someone on the fire escape.

*(***MARK** *grabs the palette knife and rushes to the windows)*

CRAIG

Hold it! Police!

*(***CRAIG** *displays a police badge)*

MARK

(Putting down the knife)

What the hell are you doing out there?

CRAIG

(Entering the apartment)

Mind if I come in?
MARK
You already are in. Maybe you could use the door next time, instead of sneaking around on the fire escape, and scaring the hell out of us!
CRAIG
You should have that windowpane fixed, Miss Conway. You know there's a serial rapist on the loose.
BRET
How do you know my name?
CRAIG
I've been working on a case involving the previous tenant. I'm Detective Russell Craig, with the Cayuga Police Department.
BRET
You're the man who's been watching this house.
MARK
Just what do you want?
CRAIG
Do you live here now, Mr. Ryder?
MARK
No -- but you probably already knew that, Detective, since you've apparently been spying on us.
BRET
Do you two know each other?
MARK
Detective Craig was the one who interviewed me when Sandy left town.

CRAIG
I'd like to ask you a few questions, Miss Conway -- if you don't mind. I won't take up much of your time.
MARK
She doesn't have to answer any questions. Especially from some cop who sneaks around on fire escapes.
CRAIG
Does she have a reason not to answer, Mr. Ryder?

MARK
There's nothing we know, that you don't already know, Detective. Look, I'm going to be late for class. Come on, Bret. We'll walk the detective out.

BRET

It's all right, Mark. I want to help in anyway I can. We can have dinner at the Hillside after your class.

MARK

I'd better stay.

CRAIG

There's no need to, Mr. Ryder. I wouldn't want you to miss your class.

BRET

Go on. I'll meet you later.

MARK

All right.

(HE *exits* DR, *closing the door as he leaves*)

CRAIG

I imagine Mr. Ryder wasn't too happy when you moved out of his apartment, and into this one.

BRET

I'm not sure that's any of your business.

CRAIG

(*Noticing the painting*)

Interesting painting. A man stalking a woman.

BRET

Is that how you see it?

CRAIG

Where did you get the idea?

BRET

Violence is all around us, Detective. It permeates our lives, affects our emotions. I put my feelings into my paintings – that's all.

CRAIG

Feelings often lead us to the truth.

BRET

You didn't come here to discuss art, now did you, Detective?

CRAIG

No. I came here to discuss Miss Barker's disappearance. You wouldn't know anything about that, would you?

BRET

Just that she may never have left town.

CRAIG

Why do you say that?

BRET

Because that's her suitcase.

(Indicating the suitcase)

I saw her the night before she was leaving. She had that all packed. And just today it turned up in the hallway outside my apartment door.

CRAIG

(Putting on a pair of gloves, opening the suitcase, and looking inside)

To your knowledge, has anyone else touched it?

BRET

Eric, my neighbor, brought it in. And, of course, whoever returned it would have touched it. What do you think it means?

KNOCKING *is heard at the door* DR.

*(***BRET** *crosses to the door and opens it)*

ERIC

(Standing in the doorway)

I hate to bother you, but you see, I'm transporting one of my constructions, and I can't turn it in the hallway without sticking part of it into your apartment.

BRET

(Looking into the hallway)

I see what you mean.

*(Opening the door wide ,*SHE *moves out of* HIS *way)*

Bring it in.

ERIC

Thanks.

*(***ERIC** *enters, dragging a large trunk-shaped object all the way into the apartment)*

CRAIG

(Removing HIS *gloves)*

Mr. Soames.

ERIC

Detective Craig! Back to ask more questions?

CRAIG

That's right. Could I help you with that? It looks heavy.

ERIC

It isn't.

CRAIG

(Crossing, then lifting one end of the object, testing the weight.)

I must be getting out of shape. It seems heavy to me. You know,

I'm becoming quite interested in art. Would you mind if I take a look?

ERIC

Do you have a warrant to investigate my art, Detective?

CRAIG

Do I need one?

ERIC

Just do me a favor and don't try to critique it. I don't think I could stomach a cop's opinion of my art.

(**ERIC** *pulls back the lid so* **CRAIG** *can see inside.* **CRAIG** *peers inside, then looks up at* **ERIC**)

CRAIG

Thank you, Mr. Soames. Since you don't want my opinion, that relieves me of one unpleasant task.

ERIC

(Closing the lid)

I think I can take it from here, Detective. . . . Thanks, Bret. Another time.

(**ERIC** *exits*, DR, *dragging the trunk-shaped object into the hallway*)

BRET

(Closing the door)

Yes, another time.

CRAIG

I must be old-fashioned, but I think art should be beautiful.

BRET

Art should reflect the soul.

CRAIG

(Spotting the nightgown on the floor. Embarrassed, **BRET** *picks it up)*

A gift from Mr. Ryder?

BRET

Yes, not that it's any of your business.

CRAIG

(Holding HIS *hand out for the nightgown.*

May I?

BRET

Reluctantly handing HIM *the nightgown)*

If it will make your day.

CRAIG

(Examining the nightgown)

Silk, is it?

*(*HE *hands the nightgown back to* **BRET***)*
Thank you.
> **BRET**
> *(Wryly)*

You don't need it for evidence? I'm sorry. I guess I haven't been
of much help.
> **CRAIG**

On the contrary. My visit here has been extremely rewarding. It
brought me to you.

> **BRET**

And of what interest am I to you?
> **CRAIG**

Does the name Henry White mean anything to you?
> **BRET**

No. Should it?
> **CRAIG**

He went on a rape-murder spree in Texas a couple of years ago.
> **BRET**

Yes, I remember now. He murdered eight women, didn't he?
> **CRAIG**

At least. I was with Houston Homicide then. Henry White was
my last case before I came here. I remember looking at his first
victim and something stirred in me -- a sense of why he'd done it.
Every time I saw a new victim, that feeling grew -- as if in some
hazy part of my mind I knew how the killer thought, who he was,
but couldn't conjure up the face. In the end, those thoughts
brought me to Henry White.

> **BRET**

What does this have to do with Sandy?
> **CRAIG**

Did you know Mr. Ryder and Sandy Barker were lovers?
> **BRET**

Why do you say that?
> **CRAIG**

Why else would he have given her such a romantic token of his
affection? A silky black nightgown. Just like the one he's given
you.
> **BRET**

No --

CRAIG

It was delivered the last night she was seen. And yet, that nightgown was never found among her effects. Do you want to know why? Because she's *buried* in that nightgown.

BRET

What?!

CRAIG

Yes! I believe she was murdered! Right here — in this very apartment.

BRET

Murdered?!

CRAIG

There's a serial rapist out there. It's not a leap of imagination to assume the rapist has turned killer – just like Henry White did. Just like Mark Ryder has.

BRET

Just like -- ?! What are you saying? That Mark -- ? You're wrong! Mark was in Syracuse when Sandy disappeared.

CRAIG

No one remembers seeing Mr. Ryder at that conference until Saturday morning. He would have had plenty of time.

BRET

It's impossible!

CRAIG

I'm just following my instincts, Miss Conway.

BRET

Well, you're on the wrong track, Detective. I know Mark.

CRAIG

Just like you knew about his affair? Don't trust Mr. Ryder. Least of all because you think you know him. People are never who they seem.

(Quickly writing a number on his card and handing it to **BRET***)*

I want to protect you, Miss Conway. I'll be watching when I can. Here's my number. You can reach me day or night.

(Putting on his gloves, HE picks up the suitcase)

I'll take this with me as evidence.

(Crossing to the apartment door DR)

Get the landlord to replace that windowpane. Keep those windows and this door locked. And don't have any further contact with Mr. Ryder.

BRET

Is that official advice, Detective?

CRAIG

Do as I ask.   I like you.   I'd hate it if next time I'm here it's because *you're* missing.

(*HE exits DR, closing the door.* **BRET** *quickly crosses to the door and locks it, then crosses to the fire escape windows and locks them. She then crosses to and picks up the full-length black nightgown*)

BRET

(*Dropping the nightgown*)

Oh, God!   Oh, God -- no!   It can't be.   Not Mark.   I know he couldn't!

KNOCKING *is heard at the apartment door* DR.

GILL

(*Off*)

Bret!   It's me!   Gill.   Are you there?

BRET

Gillian!

(**BRET** *rushes to the apartment door* DR, *unlocks and opens it*)

GILL

(*Entering* DR)

Well, it's all over.   Alec booted me out after I told him he was dull, dull, dull.   Not very nice of me, I suppose, but it's true.

(*Becoming aware of* **BRET'S** *concern*)

What's the matter?

BRET

Oh, my God, Gill!

GILL

What is it?

BRET

A police detective was just here.   He thinks -- He thinks Mark murdered Sandy!

GILL

Mark?!   That's absurd.

BRET

Is it?   Mark was here tonight full of apologies.   He said he'd been working with Sandy on his book those nights when he came home late.   That he didn't want me to misunderstand.   That's why he didn't tell me about it.   I wanted to believe him.   I did believe him. . . .   And then Detective Craig comes along and now I find out that Mark might be lying to me -- lying about those nights. Lying about being in Syracuse. Lying about Sandy! And I have to wonder . . . why all the lies?

GILL

Listen, I wouldn't jump to any conclusions. At least, not until you have some proof.

BRET

(Showing the nightgown)

Then how do you explain this? It's from Mark.

GILL

(Taking the nightgown)

An erotic peace offering?

BRET

This is serious, Gill.

GILL

(Holding the nightgown up to HER *body)*

It looks serious to me. A lot of men send black nighties to their intended victims.

BRET

Sandy was expecting someone the last night she was here. She was wearing a black nightgown -- just like this -- given to her by Mark.

GILL

After a pause)

Mark may be guilty of cheating on you, Bret. But I can't believe he's involved in murder.

BRET

But why did Mark lie to me about Sandy?

GILL

He didn't want to lose you, that's why. He loves you, in case you hadn't noticed.

BRET

Is that why he slept with Sandy? Because he loves me?

GILL

He made a mistake. That doesn't make him a murderer. You don't really think Mark would hurt anyone, do you?

BRET

He's hurt me. His lies hurt me. . . . Still, I can't believe. . . I don't want to believe. . .

GILL
Neither can I.
BRET
Despite his temper?
GILL
Mark has a hot streak, all right. I might call it impetuous, maybe even passionate. But I wouldn't call it dangerous.
(Picking the nightgown up)
Ask him what he meant by this. I'll bet he intended to utilize it in some creative way, that would have resulted in you screaming -- in pleasure, not in pain.

BRET
(Thoughtfully)
You know, Mark seemed bothered when I showed him that nightgown tonight. Almost as if -- as if he thought someone else had given it to me.
GILL
Someone else? *Is* there anyone else I should know about?
BRET
Do you think someone else *could have* given it to me? I mean, the note was typed, and it wasn't even signed. I just assumed it had come from Mark. But maybe it's from whoever's been watching me!

GILL
Don't go crazy on me, Sweetie. No one is watching you. I'm sure there's a reasonable explanation for all of this.
BRET
What is it, then?
GILL
I don't know. But I don't think you should be alone. Now that Alec has so politely asked me to leave, I could move in here with you, if you want me to.
BRET
Oh, Gill, could you? No one would dare try anything with the two of us here.
GILL
Sure. I'm not afraid of the big bad wolf.
BRET
You're wonderful.

GILL

I'll move in tomorrow -- okay?

BRET

Couldn't you stay tonight?

GILL

Tonight? I have a rendezvous with the most gorgeous man I've ever met.

(Recognizing the depth of **BRET'S** *anxiety)*

But there are other gorgeous men. Sure, I'll move in tonight. We'll have to pick up my things at Alec's.

BRET

(Replacing the nightgown in its box, and putting the box back in the dresser drawer, then closing the drawer)

I have a little time before I have to be at work at the art library. And I was supposed to meet Mark.

GILL

It won't take long. I never really unpacked from Europe. My life is still in suitcases.

(SHE picks up her coat, and crosses to the hallway door, DR)

BRET

(Putting on HER *coat)*

We can't let the landlord know you're moving in. I'm not sure he'd agree to it.

GILL

Let me break the news to him gently -- *after* I've moved in. I'll charm the pants off him.

BRET

That I'd like to see.

(THEY exit DR.

(The full-length mirror slowly opens, like a door. **HAROLD** *enters the apartment through the mirror-door, closing the door behind him. He crosses to the windows and carefully looks out, making sure that the women are leaving.*

(HE crosses to the dresser unhesitatingly and opens the top left-hand drawer of the dresser. He pulls out and opens the lingerie box. He is excited at the sight of the black nightgown which he slowly lifts from the box. He holds the nightgown in front of his face, then caresses it against his face, closing his eyes in ecstasy. Carrying the nightgown in his arms as if he were carrying a body, he crosses to the bed. He places the nightgown on the bed as if placing a body on the bed, then he straddles the

nightgown)

BLACKOUT.
END *of* SCENE THREE

[There is a minimal time interval. Eerie music is played between scenes]

ACT ONE -- SCENE FOUR

It is later the same evening.

The lamp next to the convertible couch dimly LIGHTS *the apartment. The mirror door is open.*
(HAROLD *is lying on the bed, holding the nightgown)*
The downstairs door is heard BANGING *shut.*
(HAROLD *bolts upright)*
BRET
(Off)
This suitcase is heavy!
GILL
(Off)
Not much further.
(HAROLD *quickly crams the nightgown into the box, then shoves the box into the drawer where he found it. He closes the drawer, but not completely. He exits through the mirror-door, closing it behind him. Having unlocked the apartment door,* DR, **BRET** *and* **GILL** *enter, struggling with the weight of the suitcases.* **BRET** *drops her suitcase to the floor and then turns on the overhead light)*
The room BRIGHTENS.
BRET
Oh! Thank God we made it.
(BRET *is immediately uneasy)*
I feel like someone's just been here. It's that feeling again -- of being watched.
(SHE crosses to look out the window)
GILL
(Depositing the suitcase on the bed and her purse next to the bed)
I think that detective's made you paranoid.

BRET

One thing's for sure; the landlord hasn't been here.   This windowpane is still missing.

(**BRET** *crosses to the desk and turns on the desk lamp*)

A dim LIGHT *emanates from the lamp.*

GILL

(Starting to unpack the suitcase on the bed)

I'll get the other things I left at Alec's tomorrow.   He said he didn't mind them being there -- it was just me he minded.   I guess that's what's known as a mutual parting.

BRET

You can store the suitcases in the attic after you've unpacked. The stairs are right next to Eric's apartment.

GILL

Eric? Who's that?

BRET

He lives in the apartment across the hall.

GILL

Oh yes – the one who bangs away all night.   And just what does this Eric look like?

BRET

Hands off, Gill. He's been very helpful, and I don't want you to get him all excited.

GILL

And why not? Do we have a little romance brewing?

BRET

I just met him.   Besides, you have to be careful about sleeping with strangers these days.

GILL

Oh, you've never slept with a stranger in your life, Bret.

BRET

(Noticing that the chest drawer is slightly open)

Someone *has* been here.

GILL

How do you know?

BRET

(Crossing to the chest)

This drawer is open. I'm sure I didn't leave it open.

GILL

How can you be so sure?

BRET

I'm not. I'm not sure of anything anymore.

GILL

I'm going to put this in the attic.

BRET

(Glancing nervously at her watch)

I'm going to take a quick shower before I go.

*(***BRET*** *exits into the dressing area.* ***GILL*** *exits* DR *with the suitcase, leaving the apartment door open. After a beat,* **ERIC** *knocks at the open doorway* DR, *and enters)*

ERIC

Hello? Anyone home?

(Hearing no response, HE *crosses into the apartment where he stands, casually looking about the apartment)*

> **ERIC** *is dressed as before, except he is also wearing a black leather jacket.*

GILL

(Entering DR, *and immediately seeing* **ERIC***)*

Hello. Who are you?

ERIC

I'm sorry if I startled you. The door was open, so I thought I'd drop by.

GILL

(Sizing HIM *up appreciatively)*

I bet you're Eric.

ERIC

You have the advantage.

GILL

I usually do. My name's Gillian.

ERIC

You're a friend of Bret's, I take it?

GILL

I'm staying with her for a few days.

*(***GILL*** *crosses to the wine bottle)*

What about you?

ERIC

Just being a friendly neighbor.

GILL

And how friendly is that?

ERIC

Well, that depends. I just stopped by to see about having a drink.

GILL

(Holding up the wine bottle, offering **ERIC** *a drink)*

You could join me.

ERIC

I meant, I wanted to take Bret out.

BRET

(Off)

Gill? Who are you talking to?

GILL

Your friendly neighbor.

BRET

(Off)

I'll be right out.

GILL

I think she has a date with her boyfriend.

ERIC

That excitable fellow I met earlier?

GILL

I don't know how truly excitable he is. I never had the chance to find out.

ERIC

I bet it wouldn't be hard for you.

GILL

Oh, I bet it *would.*

ERIC

You're very sure of yourself.

GILL

Don't you appreciate bold women?

ERIC

I do. In the right circumstances.

GILL

Sandy was right. You are a tough nut to crack.

ERIC

Sandy . . . ? You mean Sandy Barker? She didn't know anything about me.

GILL

Just two strangers passing on the stairs? Sometimes strangers can get to know so much about each other.

ERIC

What did she tell you?

GILL

She called you the Man in Black. You kept her awake at night --
with all of your mysterious noises.

(Indicating the direction of Eric's apartment)

Just what are you doing in there anyway?

ERIC

If I wanted you to know, I'd have invited you in. Tell Bret I'll
stop by later when she's free.

GILL

I'm not sure I like the idea of being runner-up.

ERIC

Somehow that doesn't surprise me.

GILL

Pity. I want to surprise you. Maybe that can be arranged
sometime?

ERIC

Then it wouldn't be a surprise, would it?

*(*HE *exits* DR.

*(***BRET** *enters from the dressing area)*

> SHE *is wearing a robe over her bra and panties.*

BRET

Is he gone already?

GILL

I'm sure he'll be back. I can see why you want to keep him all to
yourself.

BRET

(Removing HER *robe, and starting to dress)*

Gill. I told you -- I hardly know him.

GILL

Well, I could sure crawl all over him. He has a sort of brooding
charm, doesn't he? Who knows what lurks beneath all that black?

BRET

Do you think you can survive if you don't sleep with him?

GILL

That's a tough question.

BRET

All right, so I *am* interested in him, Gill. *Interested.* That's all.

GILL

I knew it. What about Mark?

BRET

Mark doesn't need to know about Eric right now.

GILL

I meant -- can I sleep with Mark if you're going to dump him?

BRET

You're impossible, Gill!

GILL

Just kidding.

(*Picking up the black nightgown*)

You still could give this to me. I've always looked great in black.

BRET

(*Donning* HER *parka*)

I'll be home late. Lock the door behind me.

GILL

I'm not afraid of the big, bad wolf.

BRET

Gill -- please -- humor me.

(**GILL** *shrugs and crosses to the door* DR *as* **BRET**, *carrying her purse, exits.*   **GILL** *then closes the door and starts to lock it, then purposely doesn't.*   SHE *hums as she crosses to and picks up the nightgown and holds it in front of her body, moving upstage to admire her image in the mirror*)

GILL

A shame to waste this.

(*Humming,* **GILL** *exits into the dressing area with the nightgown*)

LIGHT *from the dressing area casts her shadow while she changes into the nightgown.*

(*Off, singing*)

Who's afraid of the Big Bad Wolf,

The Big Bad Wolf,

The Big Bad Wolf?

Who's afraid of the Big Bad Wolf so early in the evening?

Bret's afraid of the Big Bad Wolf,

The Big Bad Wolf,

The Big Bad Wolf.

Bret's afraid of the Big Bad Wolf so early in the evening.

(**GILL** *reënters wearing the nightgown. She has left her street clothes in the dressing area. She briefly admires herself in front of the mirror,*

continuing to sing saucily)
I'm not afraid of the Big Bad Wolf,
The Big Bad Wolf,
The Big Bad Wolf.
I'm not afraid of the Big Bad Wolf so early in the evening.

(As SHE *sings, she crosses to and opens wide the apartment door* DR, *singing louder as she directs her voice toward Eric's apartment. She stops singing, listening for a response from Eric's apartment. Hearing none, she calls out)*
Well, I'm not afraid of you!

(SHE crosses to the bed and begins unpacking, having left the door open. (MARK appears at the doorway DR, *where he stands for a moment, watching* **GILL***)*
> HE *is dressed as earlier.*
> **MARK**
Looks like you've made yourself at home. As usual, Gill.
> **GILL**
> *(Startled)*
Mark! . . . Do you always sneak up on a woman?

*(***MARK** *crosses into the room, dropping his briefcase onto the floor at the doorway)*
> **MARK**
Only when she's parading around like that. . . . Is that Bret's nightgown?
> **GILL**
She didn't want your little peace offering. But I thought I'd give it a try.
> **MARK**
I didn't give that to Bret.
> **GILL**
Are you saying it's from someone else, then?
> **MARK**
I'm saying it sure as hell isn't from me!
> **GILL**
Really?
> **MARK**
Where is she -- in the bathroom?
> **GILL**
No -- she's gone for the evening.

MARK

Gone? But I was supposed to meet her. We were going out for dinner. I don't see how she could have forgotten about me.

GILL

You know what they say -- out of sight, out of mind. I'm sure you've felt that way -- once or twice.

MARK

What are you getting at? Where *is* Bret? . . . She's with that neighbor of hers, isn't she? That Eric! I saw him in here, trying to impress her with that phony bohemian act.

GILL

(Reclining on the bed)

Why shouldn't she be with someone else?

MARK

(Frantically crossing to the apartment door, DR*)*

Where are they? What are they doing?

GILL

If I hadn't had sex in two months, I know what I'd be doing.

MARK

(Turning on HER *angrily)*

You have no idea what it means to really love someone, do you? To want and need someone who doesn't want or need you. . . . It's like starving, it hurts so much. . . . But the pain doesn't change anything. What I do doesn't change anything.

GILL

There's nothing wrong with wanting to be wanted.

MARK

No – nothing wrong. Except when the person you *really* want no longer cares.

GILL

Well, sex with an enthusiastic partner can sure cure a lot of things – don't you agree?

MARK

(Staring at **GILL**, HIS *anger turning to interest)*

It's been a long time since I've felt that way.

GILL

I'm sure it'll come back to you.

MARK

(Crossing hesitantly to **GILL** *on the bed, staring at the nightgown)*

Are you?

GILL

We're all capable of all sorts of things – under the right circumstances.

MARK

It's been a long time since I've seen a woman in something like that.

GILL

I think it was given to the wrong woman.

(**MARK** *hesitantly bends over* **GILL**, *but* **GILL** *speaks before he can kiss her*)

You should have given it to Sandy.

MARK

(Pulling away suddenly)

Sandy?

GILL

Oh, come on, Mark. You can cut the loyal boyfriend act. I know all about you sleeping with Sandy. Sandy told me before I left for Europe.

MARK

Sandy told you? And I suppose I've got you to thank for telling Bret. I suppose that's why she's not here.

GILL

I wouldn't do that to Bret. Detective Craig told her, and she believes at least *that* part of his story.

MARK

And what was the other part of the good detective's story?

GILL

He thinks that someone gave Sandy a black nightgown, too. He thinks that whoever did that -- murdered her.

MARK

Murdered her? . . . . They've found her?

GILL

No. But that doesn't seem to matter to Detective Craig. He still thinks you killed her.

MARK

Me?! Killed Sandy? Just because I gave her a damn black nightgown?

GILL

So you *did* give her a black nightgown.

MARK

Yes! Yes! But that doesn't mean anything!

GILL

It means something to Bret. Now even *she* suspects you.

MARK

I can't believe this! This isn't happening! For all anyone knows Sandy is still alive -- out there somewhere -- anywhere! Bret can't really believe I murdered her! . . . Sandy just disappeared, for God's sake!

GILL

And you never cared what happened to her?

MARK

Yes! No! There was a time when I cared . . . when I thought I really had to know -- what could possibly have happened? But in time, I didn't *want* to know. I was glad she was just -- gone.

GILL

You were glad?

MARK

I never wanted to hurt Bret. I never wanted her to find out about the affair. What Sandy and I had was never love -- for either of us. When I finally came to my senses, I broke it off with Sandy. I swear, I haven't seen her in over a month.

GILL

That would seem noble, except she's been missing for nearly that long.

MARK

Christ! They can't really believe I murdered Sandy!

GILL

If you had only been honest with Bret from the beginning you wouldn't be in this mess.

MARK

Honest? And just what should I have told Bret? That I wanted her *and* Sandy. Do you think Bret would have appreciated my honesty?

GILL

She deserves to know the truth.

MARK

The truth is I slept with Sandy because I liked it. Liked feeling her desire. Being wanted again. Do you know how it made me feel? Powerful. Like I was in control.

(**GILL** *begins to laugh*)
Why are you laughing?
(**GILL'S** *laughter grows*)
Are you laughing at me?

GILL

In control? Is that how you felt? Did you really think all that humping between the sheets was going to be enough to satisfy Sandy?

MARK

Shut up!

GILL

You thought so! You thought all she wanted was *you*, didn't you? You never really knew what you were up against.

MARK

I was the one who ended it. Not Sandy.

GILL

But Sandy never let anyone forget the things she'd done for them. Like all that work she did on your book. Did you really think she did that for love? To help *you*?

MARK

What did she tell you about my book?

GILL

All that research she did, all that revising. Did you really expect she'd let you take all the credit? *She* was the one who was in control, you poor baby. . . . Or did you finally figure that out?

MARK

Will you shut up about Sandy! I just want to forget about her! I wish she had never existed!

GILL

And now -- she doesn't.

MARK

I didn't kill her!

GILL

What was it? Did she threaten to go to the dean? That would be just like her.

MARK

I said I didn't kill her! I don't know where she is!
(*Grabbing the desk chair,* HE *seems about to throw it at* **GILL**)
        The sound of loud BANGING *is heard off,* DR.
(*Cognizant of the noise,* **MARK** *suddenly turns, and hurls the chair far*

upstage)

You go to hell, Gill! You just go to hell!

(**MARK** *angrily grabs his coat and crosses toward the* DR *door, forgetting his briefcase.* **GILL** *stares after* **MARK,** *then rushes to close and lock the* DR *door)*

GILL

Oh, my God! My God!

(SHE *turns off the overhead light and hurriedly crosses to the alcove windows and peeks out to the street below)*

      The desk lamp dimly LIGHTS *the room. The area where the fire escape window and wall mirror are is in darkness)*

(*Determinedly,* SHE *crosses to the desk, then dials, and speaks into the phone)*

Cayuga Police Department? . . . I want to speak to Detective Craig.. . . Craig is on leave? Since when? . . . For the past *month*?! Then who the hell is investigating the murder of Sandy Barker? . . . There *is* no murder investigation?

    *(*SHE *hangs up)*

What the hell are you after, *Detective* Craig? . . . I've got to find Bret.

(**GILL** *quickly exits into the dressing area,* DR.

(*A* FIGURE *enters, as if emerging from the shadows, from the upstage corner of the room where both the full-length mirror and the fire escape windows are located. It has been impossible to make out the precise point of entry.*

      The FIGURE *wears dark outer clothing and a black ski mask.*

(*The* FIGURE *approaches the stage right dressing area door, but quickly backs up against the wall, into the shadows, when* **GILL** *reënters, carrying her clothes. The* FIGURE *quickly and quietly approaches her from behind. Sensing its presence,* **GILL** *turns to face it. But before she can scream, the* FIGURE *grabs her throat and begins strangling her. As the* FIGURE *strangles her, it pushes her down onto the bed)*

BLACKOUT.

<u>END *of* ACT ONE</u>

ACT TWO -- SCENE ONE

It is later that night. The DR *apartment door and the upstage fire escape windows are open. The mirror-door is open. The side table and lamp that were next to the open couch-bed, and the black nightgown, lie on the floor. Gill's purse is on the floor next to the bed.*
The bedside lamp is ON. *The overhead light is* OFF.
During the following action, the BELLS *from the university's clock tower can be heard striking eleven.*

(**HAROLD** *is in Bret's apartment. He returns the side table to its upright position, then sets the lamp on the table*)

HE *is dressed as he was in Act I, Scene 4. A tape measure is hooked to one back pocket, and a flashlight to the other. A screwdriver sticks out of a back pocket.*

(**HAROLD**, *scanning the room, notices Gill's coat. He picks it up, and carries it to the mirror/doorway, placing it inside the passageway and closing the mirror/door. He crosses to the open fire escape windows and closes them. He glances about, to see if anything else is amiss. He crosses DR, drawn by the black nightgown lying on the floor. He picks up the nightgown, treating it as something both frightening and arousing*)

There are SOUNDS *from off,* DR.

(**HAROLD** *drops the nightgown, turns the table lamp off, and darts out the apartment door,* DR, *taking care to close the door very quietly*)

BRET
(Off)
Who is it? . . . Mr. Lemb!
HAROLD
(Off)
I have my tape measure here. I came to measure that broken pane.
BRET
(Entering DR, *turning on the overhead light*)
This late?

The room is now brightly LIT.

HAROLD

(Also entering, DR, *not closing the door)*

I'm only thinking of you, Miss Conway -- of your safety. I thought you were afraid someone might climb in through those fire escape windows. Well, shall I measure that pane or not?

BRET

All right. . . . It's just that -- it's just that a girlfriend is spending a few nights here with me.

HAROLD

I know about her already.

BRET

You know about Gill?

HAROLD

I've seen her.

(With alarm, HE *notices Gill's purse, which* **BRET** *does not see)*

BRET

I know your rule about no overnight guests.

(Calling into the kitchenette/dressing area)

Gill?

*(***HAROLD** *crosses toward the purse, but stops when* **BRET** *turns to speak)*

I planned to tell you.

(Hurrying into the kitchenette/dressing area at stage right.

Gill?

*(***HAROLD** *quickly picks up the purse and crosses hurriedly to the mirror door. He opens the door, puts the purse inside and closes the door just as* **BRET** *reënters.* **BRET** *is concerned over* GILL'S *absence)*

HAROLD

She's gone.

BRET

You saw her leave? But she said she was going to stay in for the night.

HAROLD

She didn't.

BRET

Did she happen to say anything? Where she was going?

HAROLD

Why would she? You both thought you were fooling me, didn't you?

BRET

We didn't intend to mislead you, Mr. Lemb.

HAROLD

I know what you intended.

BRET

Well, the truth is, I was scared to be here alone. Did you know the police think Sandy Barker was murdered?

HAROLD

I wouldn't believe everything Detective Craig says.

BRET

How do you know what Detective Craig told me?

HAROLD

That was him on the street yesterday. I knew it was only a matter of time, before he'd want to meet you face to face.

BRET

I thought you didn't know who that man was.

HAROLD

I know him. He was here -- asking questions about Miss Barker's personal life, questions I couldn't possibly know the answers to. It's all something I want to forget.

BRET

I wouldn't have moved in here if I'd known the police suspected Sandy had been murdered.

HAROLD

That detective . . . he told me Miss Barker was missing. That's all. I was just as surprised as you were to learn he suspected that – your friend with the temper killed her.

BRET

How do you know that?

HAROLD

I make it my business to know what goes on in this house. If you're going to be suspicious of anyone, it should be of that boyfriend of yours. He came here the night Miss Barker was supposed to leave.

BRET

Mark was here that night?

HAROLD

That's right. And then he stopped coming -- until you moved in. He was here tonight -- with your girlfriend.

(During the following conversation, **ERIC** *appears outside the open*

doorway DR. *He unlocks his apartment door, enters his apartment, leaving the door open, then reenters the hallway and listens outside Bret's door. The* OTHERS *do not see him)*

BRET

Mark was here with Gill?

HAROLD

That's right. Just like he used to be here with Miss Barker all those nights.

BRET

No. He was at the restaurant. He was supposed to meet me.

HAROLD

He was here. They were here. On the bed.

BRET

(Reacting painfully to the news)

On the bed?

HAROLD

(Pointing to the black nightgown)

She was wearing that.

BRET

You *saw* them together?

HAROLD

He was pushing ... pushing her down ... down to the bed.

BRET

You saw that? How? How did you see that? *Where* were you?

HAROLD

Where? ... I was ... I was ...

BRET

In your favorite hiding place?

HAROLD

What do you mean! I saw them when I came to measure the pane. I -- I don't spy on my tenants, if that's what you mean!

BRET

Then why are you always in that hallway outside my door?

HAROLD

This is my house! I can do whatever I want! You can always leave if you don't like it here.

BRET

That won't stop me from asking questions.

HAROLD

You better watch it, Miss Conway. I don't think you really want to know the answers to those questions -- what I've seen.

ERIC

(Appearing outside the open door and knocking)

Bret? Could I intrude again? I've got to move this empty crate back into my apartment.

BRET

(Relieved to see **ERIC***)*

Please come in.

*(***ERIC** *drags in the large trunk-shaped crate, which he places* DR *near the doorway)*

ERIC

Oh, Harold. What are you doing here? Isn't it past your bedtime?

HAROLD

I'm finished for now.

*(*HE *exits* DR*)*

BRET

Have you seen Gill?

ERIC

(Crossing just into the hallway to open his apartment door and then dragging the trunk inside, closing the door and returning to **BRET'S** *apartment)*

Not since earlier -- when you were in the shower.

BRET

She said she was staying in -- unpacking. But her coat and purse are gone.

ERIC

Maybe she just decided to go out, on the spur of the moment.

BRET

Maybe that's not all she decided to do on the spur of the moment.

(Having noticed Mark's briefcase, **BRET** *picks it up)*

Harold wasn't lying. . . . Mark *has* been here. This is his.

ERIC

I heard what Harold said about Mark and Gill. Would Mark really do that to you?

BRET

It wouldn't be the first time.

ERIC

Then he's a fool.

BRET

I'm not sure who's the fool.

ERIC

I know how hard it is — when people you care about aren't who you thought they were. . . . I know how much it hurts. . . . I've been there.

BRET

(Reflective pause)

Maybe — maybe it's time I realized — that I don't know Mark — that maybe I never knew him . . .

ERIC

What really brought you to this apartment? What did you think you'd find?

BRET

If Mark and Sandy were still seeing each other. I just wanted to know the truth.

ERIC

Well maybe you've discovered more than you wanted to know.

BRET

(After a beat)

Detective Craig thinks Mark is the rapist who's been attacking women around here. He thinks – he thinks Mark killed Sandy.

ERIC

What? He really believes that? . . . And you're beginning to believe it, too? Because of what Harold told you about Mark and Sandy? I'm not sure I would trust much of what Harold tells you.

BRET

It's not just that.

ERIC

You know, Craig practically accused me of murdering Sandy.

BRET

Why would he do that?

ERIC

Because I was alone working in my apartment the night she was last seen. Who knows what Craig's thinking? If you want my opinion, I think he gets off on convincing pretty, young women that he's protecting them from some evil out there.

BRET

(Sarcastically)

Well, that makes me feel better. And I thought Harold was scary.

(After a beat, seriously)

Harold knows things about me -- things that he couldn't possibly know.   It's as if he's been in this apartment -- watching.   He knows everything that people do and say in here.

ERIC

What does he know?

BRET

He knew Detective Craig had been here to see me -- and I get the feeling he knew exactly what the detective said to me.   He knew Gill moved in.   He knew what she was wearing.

ERIC

There's nothing ominous about any of that.   I knew Craig had been here to see you.   I knew Gill had moved in.   Does that make me scary?

BRET

No.

ERIC

If you're really nervous about Harold, I could stay here with you tonight . . . that is, if you want me to . . .

(Glancing at the couch that is already unfolded — now a double bed)

. . . on the couch, of course.   Do you think you could sleep -- with me here?

BRET

(Still distracted)

I'm too keyed up to sleep.   . . . But I guess I really don't want to be alone.

ERIC

Well, then, we could stay up all night.   And talk.   Or . . . we could -- play cards.

BRET

(Taking HIM seriously)

Cards? I'm afraid I only know War and Hearts.

ERIC

I know all kinds of games.   I'm good at ones with partners.

BRET

But there are only two of us.

ERIC

I think we can work something out.   . . . I'm an expert.

BRET

(Finally getting HIS intent)

An expert?
>   **ERIC**
>   *(Approaching* HER*)*

Should I get out that deck of cards?
>   **BRET**

I wouldn't want you to take advantage of me. It's been a while since I played. I'm afraid I wouldn't be any good.
>   **ERIC**

It's like swimming. You never forget. You just dive in and stroke.
>   **BRET**

It's never been that easy for me.
>   **ERIC**
>   *(*HE *moves another step closer to* HER*)*

You could just flow with the currents. Sometimes it's better just to let go -- to not fight.
>   **BRET**

I'm afraid.
>   **ERIC**
>   *(Touching* HER *face)*

I know you are. I've known that ever since I saw your painting. Our creations always betray us.
>   **BRET**

Do they?
>   **ERIC**

You've haunted me, Bret. Distracted me. Ever since I met you, I've thought of nothing else.
>   **BRET**

I've thought of you, too. I've wondered what you would be like . . . But I'm confused.
>   **ERIC**

I'm not confused. I know exactly what I feel. What I want.
>   *(*HE *kisses* **BRET***, and she responds only for an instant)*
>   **BRET**

I -- hardly know you.
>   **ERIC**

What better way to get acquainted?
>   *(***ERIC** *kisses* HER *again, more passionately. She hesitates at first, then responds. Their words are uttered between kisses)*

I want you to like it – what I do . . .

BRET
I -- I want to like it.

ERIC
To surrender . . .

BRET
Yes . . .

ERIC
Tell me . . .

BRET
Yes . . .

ERIC
Tell me what you like . . . what you want . . .

(ERIC gently draws **BRET** *to the bed. They kiss passionately)*

BRET
(Suddenly pulling away from HIM)
No! . . . I can't.

ERIC
What's wrong?

BRET
I just can't. I'm sorry. It wouldn't be fair.

ERIC
To Mark?

BRET
Or to you.

ERIC
That's all right. There are no "have to's."

BRET
(Pause)
But I don't want to stay here tonight. Not on that bed.

ERIC
(Holding out HIS *hand to* HER)
You can stay in my apartment.

(After a slight hesitation, **BRET** *takes* HIS *hand)*
We'll -- play cards.

(As THEY *exit,* DR, **BRET** *turns off the overhead light and closes the door)*

> *The room is in virtual darkness, the only* LIGHT *filtering in from ambient outside lighting)*

(The beam of a flashlight, originating from outside the fire escape windows, suddenly cuts through the darkness. A FIGURE, *holding the*

flashlight, enters through the fire escape window)
(The FIGURE *is* **CRAIG**, *but this is not revealed to the audience.*

> **CRAIG** *is dressed in dark pants and a dark hooded sweatshirt, his face obscured by the darkness and by a hood pulled up over his head.*

*(***CRAIG*** *begins sweeping the beam of light across the room, coming to rest on the nightgown. He crosses to the nightgown and picks it up)*

> *The phone* RINGS.

*(*HE *trains the beam of light on the telephone and crosses to it)*

> *The phone* RINGS *again and Bret's answering machine responds with the usual greeting. After the greeting,* **MARK'S** *voice is heard leaving a message.*

> **MARK'S VOICE**

Bret, please pick up. It's me – Mark.

(After a brief pause)

Please, Bret, I need to talk to you.

(After a brief pause, disconcerted)

I guess you're not there. . . . Well, call me when you get in – okay?

> *There is the* SOUND *of Mark disconnecting.*

(Still unidentifiable by the audience, **CRAIG** *removes the tape from the answering machine and slips it into his pocket)*

SLOW FADE *to* BLACK.

END *of* SCENE ONE

[There is a minimal interval between scenes]

ACT TWO -- SCENE TWO

It is around nine the next evening. The upstage fire escape windows, the apartment door DR, *and the mirror-door, are closed. The apartment appears as it had the night before, except that Gill's clothing has been removed. The couch/bed has been returned to a couch position.*

The overhead LIGHT *is* ON — *the room brightly lit.*

*(***BRET*** *is sitting on the stool in front of the easel, at stage left. She*

opens the turpentine can, pours from it into the paintbrush jar, and closes the can. She starts to paint, in a distracted manner. Only the back of the canvas she is painting on is visible to the audience)

> SHE *is dressed in a sweater and jeans. A painting shirt protects her sweater.*

> KNOCKING *is heard at the apartment door* DR.

BRET

(Crossing hurriedly to the door)

Gill? Is that you?

> *(*SHE *opens the door, where* **MARK** *is standing)*

MARK

Sorry to disappoint you. It's only me. . . . Can I come in?

> *(*HE *pushes his way in, immediately scanning the room)*

Where were you last night?

BRET

Where were you?

MARK

I was waiting for you.

BRET

At the restaurant?

MARK

Yes. Like we agreed. But you never showed up.

BRET

(Picking up HIS *briefcase)*

Then how did this get here?

MARK

I came by to get you, but I guess you had other things on your mind.

BRET

I think you're the one who had other things in mind.

MARK

What's that supposed to mean?

BRET

The landlord told me he saw you here with Gill.

MARK

I already said I was here. When I saw Gill, she was standing right there -- telling me you bought that bull Craig handed you.

> *(Holding out the folder)*

Well, I spent all day doing my own investigation of Detective Russell Craig. Do you know what I found? Craig didn't voluntarily leave the Houston Police Department. He was forced to leave.

BRET

Forced to leave?

MARK

See for yourself.

(HE *throws folder with the newspaper clippings on the bed*)

I had copies made so you'd know I was telling the truth.

(**BRET** *crosses to the bed, picks up the folder and begins reading*)

Seems Craig was so obsessed with trying to nab Henry White that he used a rookie policewoman as a decoy. But Craig was a bit slow on the surveillance. He didn't intervene until the policewoman almost became White's last victim. . . . But Craig *wanted* to make sure he caught White in the act.

BRET

Are you saying Detective Craig *purposely waited* until White hurt her before stopping him?

MARK

She has the scars to prove it. . . . It gave Craig a reason to beat a confession out of White during the arrest. But there was some question about whether White really killed all of them.

BRET

You're just saying all of this because Detective Craig is convinced *you're*

(SHE *falters*)

MARK

I'm what?

BRET

That you're . . .

(SHE *is unable to finish*)

MARK

That I'm a killer? And has he convinced you? . . . I can see that he has. Has it ever occurred to you that Craig is personally involved?

BRET

Personally involved? What do you mean?

MARK

Why does he come around here pestering you, frightening you with stories about me? Maybe so you would run to him the moment you felt danger. Run to him -- believing he would protect you. But he won't protect you, Bret -- he's a dangerous man.

BRET

You're just trying to confuse me. Where's Gill, Mark? What did you two do last night?

MARK

I don't know what you think, but nothing happened between Gill and me.

BRET

Mr. Lemb told me!

MARK

Told you what?

BRET

About you and Gill -- there! On the bed! I don't know how far you'd gotten. Far enough, according to Mr. Lemb.

MARK

It's a lie! Look, you want the truth? Gill looked pretty damn good to me last night, but I was hardly in the mood to act on any erotic impulses. I was thinking of you, fool that I am.

BRET

Are you saying she didn't go home with you?

MARK

I spent the night alone. Which is more than I can say for you. I phoned you after I was here last night -- but you weren't answering -- for some reason.

BRET

You didn't call.

MARK

I left a message on your machine. But apparently you were too busy to call me back.

BRET

Give me a break, Mark. You didn't leave a message.

MARK

You know I did. You still haven't told me what you were doing last night.

BRET

I wasn't doing anything that's any of your business!

MARK

Don't lie about this, Bret. Gill made it pretty clear that you were interested in Eric.

BRET

Do we really want to talk about lies, Mark? . . . I mean, you've become such an expert.

MARK

The last time I saw Gill she was here -- dressed for bed. . . . Wearing that black nightgown. The one I suppose Eric gave you.

BRET

You gave that nightgown to me.

MARK

Oh, please, Bret -- you know I didn't.

BRET

Have you forgotten the card? It said, "*For the woman of my dreams.*"

MARK

(Aghast)

It said what? Show me the card!

(**BRET** *finds the card and hands it to* **MARK**. *Upon reading it,* **MARK** *is agitated*)

My God . . . My God . . . You have to believe me -- I never sent you that nightgown, Bret. But I did send Sandy a black nightgown –

BRET

So you admit it – you *were* lovers.

MARK

Yes! Yes! I *did* sleep with Sandy -- a few times. I didn't want you to know, because she didn't mean anything to me. Because I love you! I love you!

BRET

I used to think I knew you. I trusted you. I used to . . .

MARK

Love me?

BRET

I did . . .

MARK

The way I still love you?

BRET

What else have you lied about?

MARK

Nothing.

BRET

Mr. Lemb told me you were here the night Sandy disappeared.

Were you here?
> **MARK**

Yes. I was here. I came to end it. But Sandy wasn't here, Bret. .
. . I know you don't believe me anymore. But you have to listen
to me! I did send Sandy a nightgown --- with this card – this *exact*
card.
> **BRET**

The *same* card?
> **MARK**
> *(HIS actual plight downing on him)*

Yes! Don't you see? I'm being set up!
> **BRET**
> *(Not believing HIM)*

Set up?
> **MARK**

For Sandy's murder!
> **BRET**

But who would have known about the nightgown – the card --
except for you and Sandy?

> **MARK**
> *(The thought occurring to HIM)*

Mr. Lemb seems to know an awful lot, doesn't he?
> **CRAIG**
> *(Off, knocking on the door DR)*

Miss Conway? . . . Miss Conway?
> **MARK**
> *(Crossing DR to the door, and opening it)*

So nice of you to use the door this time, Detective.
> **CRAIG**
> *(Entering)*

I've come to discuss something with Miss Conway -- before I
have to leave for Albany, in half an hour.

> **MARK**

Go ahead.
> **CRAIG**

In private.
> **MARK**

I don't think so, Detective. Do you really believe I'd leave Bret
alone -- with *you*?

CRAIG

Are you afraid of what I might tell her?

MARK

No.

CRAIG

Should I tell her where I found Miss Barker's purse?

MARK

Her purse?

BRET

Where did you find it?

CRAIG

Where Mr. Ryder hid it.

MARK

Where I what?

CRAIG

Where you hid it. In the closet at your office.

BRET

Oh, God.

MARK

I -- that's impossible! I didn't put that there!

CRAIG

I suppose it just appeared there, by magic.

MARK

Someone's setting me up!

CRAIG

Now who would want to do that?

MARK

Maybe you, Detective.

CRAIG

I don't need to frame you, Mr. Ryder. You're doing a pretty good job of incriminating yourself.

MARK

Or that landlord.

CRAIG

Oh – so now it's Mr. Lemb. He has access to your office, does he?

MARK

Bret -- I don't know what's happening. I don't know what happened to Sandy. If you ever believe anything I say, please believe that.

BRET

You'd better go, Mark

MARK

Is that what you really want?

(When **BRET** *doesn't answer,* **MARK** *grabs his briefcase and crosses to the* DR *hall door, then pauses)*

For your information, Bret, I don't know how Sandy's purse got into my office. And I didn't see your landlord last night. He was never in here -- at least, not while I was. That's the truth. . . .

*(***MARK** *exits, closing the door)*

BRET

How did you know to look for that purse in Mark's office, Detective?

CRAIG

An anonymous tip. Have you heard from your friend Gill?

BRET

No. Mark saw her last night. He says he left her alone here and no one's seen her since.

CRAIG

Isn't that interesting?

BRET

(Crossing to retrieve the card and handing it to **CRAIG***)*

Mark says he didn't give me that black nightgown, but it came with this card he'd sent to Sandy. What if someone else had been here the night Sandy disappeared and taken that note? What if someone else is doing this to Mark?

CRAIG

You really want to believe Mr. Ryder's frame-up story? Well, let's talk about Miss Barker's suitcase. Mr. Ryder's fingerprints are on it.

BRET

His fingerprints . . .? No . . .

CRAIG

Oh, yes. Do you still believe him?

*(***BRET** *contemplates silently)*

Who lied to you about his affair with Sandy Barker?

BRET

Mark, but --

CRAIG

Who had Sandy's purse hidden in his office?

BRET

Mark.

CRAIG

Who lied about the nightgown he gave to her?

BRET

Mark.

CRAIG

Can't you see he's lying to you still? About the nightgown he's given you? About what he's done to Miss Barker?

BRET

I *know* Mark. I lived with him, for God's sake! He's not capable of such a terrible thing!

CRAIG

Sometimes the most normal-seeming people are capable of the most horrible things.

BRET

Does that include you, Detective?

CRAIG

You know what Henry White's neighbors said about him? They said he was the nicest guy. They thought they knew *him*. Just after he killed Lonnie Gamble he told me what a heartache and a sin it was that such a sweet neighborhood girl like her could have died so horribly. And I believed him. I believed him and six more women were murdered. I believed the wrong man.

BRET

When did you stop believing? When you beat a confession out of him?

CRAIG

No. When I caught him in his basement whittling my partner with a steak knife. . . . When you look into a shark's eyes, Miss Conway, you realize you're capable of doing almost anything to stop him.

BRET

Anything?

CRAIG

I despise the Henry Whites of the world – pleading they are the tortured souls when its they who torture. . . . And now someone very like him is here.

BRET

Someone like him?

CRAIG

I thought I could leave Henry White behind. But it's as if he's traveled all this way, seeking me out like an old friend. We all have choices, Miss Conway. Sooner or later we have to own up to those choices. Sooner or later, we all have to face the truth. No matter how terrible it is.

BRET

I know the truth now. Mark had an affair. That's all! He didn't want me to know about it because he loves me.

CRAIG

It's not love he craves but having power over another human being.

Above all he needs to be in control.

BRET

He does love me!

CRAIG

Does he really? Or is he desperately afraid of losing you – afraid you'll slip away from his grasp? And if he can't have you? What is the ultimate control, the ultimate power? Taking another life. He gets to decide *when* you die. *Where* you die. *How* you die.

BRET

How *I* die?

CRAIG

He intends to kill you.

BRET

Kill me?! No! I can't believe it!

CRAIG

Don't you understand? He's already tried once. He came for you, but found Gill in your place.

BRET

Gill? . . . What are you saying?

CRAIG

Who was the last to see Gill alive?

BRET

Are you saying Mark killed Gill? You don't know Gill's dead!

CRAIG

Where is she then? If he left her safe and sound, as he claims he did -- why hasn't she called you?

(**BRET** *is silent*)

I know what obsession can lead to. It's like a ticking bomb up here.

(Pointing to HIS *head)*

Who knows what sets it off? But it's going to explode.

BRET

(Breaking down)

No! . . . No . . .

CRAIG

Don't trust him, Miss Conway. Not anymore. He needs to finish what he's started with you -- what he thought he had finished when he murdered Gill.

BRET

I can't believe it!

CRAIG

It's going to happen. In his mind, it's already set in motion. . . . But don't worry. I have a plan. . . . I want to get this guy. I want to get him for your sake -- and for Gillian's. . . . With your help, I *will* get him. And then he won't kill anybody else.

BRET

What do you want me to do?

CRAIG

Something very brave.

(Picking up the nightgown)

I need you to put this on.

BRET

What?!

CRAIG

I let it slip that I was going to Albany tonight -- remember? Mark thinks you'll be all alone. Put this on as if you think it's come from a loving boyfriend. Then go to bed. When he comes, I'll be hiding -- waiting for him.

BRET

You'll be hiding here? You want me to be a decoy?

CRAIG

This killer is clever. . . . So very clever, I need to catch him in the act.

BRET

I -- can't!

CRAIG

He's coming back whether you do this for me or not.

BRET

No!

CRAIG

I want to protect you. . . . I want to protect whoever might be next -- after you.

BRET

I said no! I won't be your decoy. I think you're the one who's obsessed, Detective. I think you *want* to believe Mark did these terrible things. Why -- I don't know. . . . But I'm not going to believe Gill's dead until I see her body!

CRAIG

She is dead.

BRET

That's what you say. But Mr. Lemb saw her leave here last night.

CRAIG

He saw her leave?

BRET

That's what he said. He said Mark and Gill were -- on the bed. But Mark said Mr. Lemb was never here. Mr. Lemb seems to know a lot of things he shouldn't. Maybe you should be talking to him.

CRAIG

It would be a mistake to believe Mr. Ryder.

BRET

(*Putting on* HER *parka*)

If you'll excuse me, Detective Craig. I'm going to go look for Gill.

CRAIG

You won't find her.

BRET

I'm still going to look.

CRAIG

(*Throwing the nightgown over the back of the couch*)

Let me go with you. You shouldn't be alone.

BRET

I think I'll be a lot safer if I *am* alone . . . Now I want you to leave.

CRAIG

You may not like how I do things -- how I think -- but in the end you'll know I was here for you.

BRET
(Holding the door open, as a signal for HIM *to leave)*
Detective.

CRAIG
(As HE *crosses to the apartment door* DR*)*
You believe people are basically good -- but it's the other way around.

BRET
Good-bye, Detective.

CRAIG
Take care, Miss Conway.

*(*HE *exits.* **BRET** *closes and locks the door, then crosses to the windows to watch him leave. She then exits into the stage right kitchen/dressing area door. When* **BRET** *reënters, she is holding a large, sharp kitchen knife which she puts into her purse. Taking her purse, she, exits* DR*)*

The LIGHTING *has become* DIMMER.

*(*HAROLD *opens the mirror-door upstage and enters. He crosses to the alcove windows and watches Bret depart.* **HAROLD** *then crosses upstage behind the couch and picks up the nightgown.*

*(*HE *holds it in his hands, transfixed by it. Then, as if overcome with hatred for the nightgown, he violently grips it in his hands. He grabs the palette knife from the easel stand and savagely rips at the nightgown with it.*

*(*CRAIG *appears on the fire escape deck and watches for a moment, then bursts through the windows, gun drawn.*

(Startled, **HAROLD** *turns toward* **CRAIG**, *raising the palette knife in a defensive and threatening manner.*

(Aiming the gun at **HAROLD***)*
Go ahead.

(After a slight hesitation, **HAROLD** *drops the palette knife.*

*(*CRAIG *grabs* **HAROLD** *and shoves him up against the wall next to the mirror/door, training the gun on him)*

HAROLD
What do you want?

CRAIG
(Frisking **HAROLD***)*
I'll ask the questions, Mr. Lemb.
(Glancing into the passageway)
Very convenient. A secret passageway that leads -- down to your

apartment, I presume.
> **HAROLD**

You can't just barge in here! You need a warrant.
> **CRAIG**

Shut up! Put your hands on your head and get over there!

> (**HAROLD** *complies as* **CRAIG** *shoves him in the direction of the couch.*

> (**CRAIG** *examines the mirror-door more carefully*)

How clever, Mr. Lemb. A see-through mirror! I guess you know practically everything that's gone on in this room.

> (*Seeing something inside the passageway*)

What's this?

> (**CRAIG** *pulls out from the passageway Gill's coat and purse and reads silently from the ID he finds inside the purse*)

These belong to Gillian Hastings.

> (*Crossing to* **HAROLD**)

> **HAROLD**

I just wanted my passageway to be safe from people like you. That's why I hid those things. But you found out anyway -- with all your prying and spying.

> **CRAIG**

I'm not the rat who's been hiding in the wall. What have you done to her?

> **HAROLD**

I never hurt anyone.

> **CRAIG**

> (*Prodding* **HAROLD** *with the gun*)

It has just occurred to me that you have. It would be better if you told me about it. Better for you, I mean.

> **HAROLD**

I swear, I only watched.

> **CRAIG**

Did you see the look of surprise in her eyes, or was it too dark? Could she see you, or was your face hidden in shadow? Can you ever forget the excitement rushing through you -- the absolute power you felt when you killed her?

> **HAROLD**

Killed her?! I never killed anyone!

> **CRAIG**

Her murder floods your mind, and you can't get rid of it. But you don't really want to get rid of it. There's something quite pleasant about it -- isn't there?

HAROLD

No! I didn't do anything!

CRAIG

But you did. I know your kind. You never think you did anything, when you've done so very much.

HAROLD

I know all about you! I know you're not really a cop anymore.

(Rising, and starting to cross toward the apartment door DR)

I know my rights!

*(**CRAIG** grabs **HAROLD**, restraining him)*

CRAIG

What makes you think you have rights?

*(**CRAIG** flings **HAROLD** to the floor)*

HAROLD

(Cowering)

You're crazy!

CRAIG

Maybe I am.

*(**CRAIG** points the gun menacingly at **HAROLD**)*

HAROLD

Don't! Please . . .

CRAIG

I'm not a patient man. I need to know what you know.

HAROLD

I didn't kill anyone! I swear!

CRAIG

*(HE fiercely pokes **HAROLD** in the stomach with his foot)*

That's not what I want to hear.

HAROLD

(Lying on the floor, in pain and fear)

All right! All right! Just don't hurt me! . . . I watched her that night. She put on a black, silky nightgown and strutted around in it, as if she knew . . .

CRAIG

. . . you were there.

HAROLD

Yes. I felt she wanted me to reach out -- to touch her. Just like the others. In the other houses. The other nights when I watched them through their unlocked windows.

CRAIG

You raped those other women.

HAROLD

Why would they leave their windows unlocked if they didn't want me to come in? If they didn't want me to . . . But I could never do that in this house . . . She turned off the light, and I watched, that's all. Watched and imagined that the darkness of her room and the darkness of my space was the same darkness -- that she and I were merged through the darkness. . . . Then he came.

CRAIG

Who came?

HAROLD

It was almost as if she knew he was there. She jumped up, as if into his arms, and for a moment I thought she wanted him. Then his hands were around her throat, squeezing . . . squeezing . . .

CRAIG

Who did you see? Who was it?

HAROLD

He came from the shadows. From the night. So close I thought he could be my own reflection. A dark reflection.

CRAIG

Who was it?

HAROLD

It could have been you.

CRAIG

Me?

HAROLD

It could have been anyone. I couldn't see his face. It was like a nightmare.

CRAIG

(Holstering HIS *gun)*

You want to believe someone else killed them, because you can't bear the thought it was you.

HAROLD

No. I never touched her. It was someone else. He killed Miss Hastings – just like he killed Miss Barker.

(Begins to laugh nervously)

But Miss Barker's not dead – not really. I've seen her – here – in these rooms. She's a ghost.

CRAIG
(**CRAIG** *grabs* **HAROLD**, *and wrestles him to a standing position*)
Don't lie to me, you son-of-a-bitch!
HAROLD
He came through the window! – Just like you --
CRAIG
It was you, you sniveling weasel!
(**CRAIG** *shakes* **HAROLD** *violently*)
It was *you*! *You* killed them!
HAROLD
No!
(**CRAIG** *hits* **HAROLD** *across the face*. **HAROLD** *crumples onto the bed*)
CRAIG
You killed them!
(**CRAIG** *continues to strike him, while* **HAROLD**, *writhing on the bed, ineffectually tries to ward off the blows*)
You! It was you! It had to be you!
HAROLD
No -- don't.
CRAIG
Just looking, and not touching can make you crazy. So you waited behind this mirror, watching them, wanting them. . . . But they didn't want you, did they? . . . It was just a fantasy -- conjured up in the dark, while you were alone with yourself, hating them for not letting you inside. But there's something quite satisfying about acting out those secret desires, isn't there? . . . Isn't there?
HAROLD
(*Quietly*)
Yes.
CRAIG
In your fantasies no one ever says no. In your fantasies they want you. They want what you do to them.
(**HAROLD** *nods, as* **CRAIG** *continues to poke and prod him*)
You'll tell me everything I want to hear, won't you! . . . Won't you!
HAROLD
Yes . . . whatever you want. Just don't hurt me anymore. Please . . .

(Prone on the bed, **HAROLD** *gropes for a weapon. His fingers happen to find the table lamp)*

CRAIG

You're all the same in the end -- whimpering and weak. What made you turn out that way? A bad mommy, not enough love? Well not everybody who's been deprived of love turns out like you. . . . Some of them turn out like me.

*(***HAROLD*** manages to grab the lamp, and hit* **CRAIG** *on the head.* **CRAIG** *slumps to his knees, momentarily stunned.* **HAROLD** *rushes upstage to the mirror passageway, disappearing inside, as* **CRAIG** *jumps up, drawing his gun)*

Stop!

*(***CRAIG*** exits into the mirror passageway)*
A SHOT *is* HEARD.
BLACKOUT.

END *of* SCENE TWO

[There is a minimal interval between scenes]

ACT TWO -- SCENE THREE

It is two hours later. The lamp by the couch/bed has been returned to its original position. The purse is gone. The apartment door DR, *the upstage fire escape windows, and the mirror-door are closed.*

The apartment is dimly LIT *by the table lamp, and outside ambient lighting.*

*(***BRET*** enters* DR, *and turns on the overhead light. She closes and locks the door)*

The room is LIT BRIGHTLY.

During the following action, the BELLS *from the university's clock tower can be heard striking eleven.*

BRET

Gill! . . . Gill, please be here.

(Hearing no response, anxiety-ridden, SHE *hurriedly checks the kitchenette/dressing area, leaving the* DR *door ajar. She reappears dejectedly, and crosses to the answering machine)*

No messages.
(Overwhelmed with guilt and sorrow)
Oh -- Gill! . . . Gill! -- where are you?
MARK
(Entering DR in a very agitated state)
Something terrible has happened!

BRET
Is it Gill? . . . What's happened?
MARK
Someone has erased my entire book from the computer in my office!
BRET
What? You mean someone -- purposely . . . ?
MARK
Gone! It's gone! Do you know what this means? My tenure . . . my career!
BRET
But you must have copies. You can . . .
MARK
They're gone! All of it's gone!
(More to HIMSELF)
She threatened to erase my book. She said she would destroy me. And now – somehow – she has.
BRET
Who?
MARK
Sandy.
BRET
Sandy's dead, Mark. Her suitcase had your fingerprints.
MARK
My fingerprints? It's not possible! You have to believe me!
BRET
I have believed you.
MARK
I don't know what's real anymore. It feels like the earth's shifting beneath me. I'm half-mad because of all of this. Because you won't return my calls. Because I've lost you! Lost everything!

BRET
You never called me.

MARK
I did! I left messages on your machine. All day today. You didn't get them?

BRET
I checked the machine just now. There aren't any messages!

MARK
But I swear!

BRET
More lies, Mark?

MARK
No! No! God, what's happening? . . . Maybe the machine's broken? Yes! That's it. It must be broken.

BRET
It's not broken!

(SHE *quickly crosses to the answering machine, and presses the message button. The machine is silent*)

See? No flashing light. No messages.

MARK
Check the tape. . . . Please!

BRET
(After opening the machine's lid, and peering inside)

It's gone!

MARK
I left my briefcase here last night. That's when the disks were stolen. You see! Someone *has* been in here!

BRET
Yes . . . I've felt it.

MARK
Don't you see? Everything's been planted! The suitcase. The purse. The nightgown. Everything pointing to me as Sandy's killer.

BRET
Yes – someone's playing some twisted game.

MARK
Trying to get you to doubt me. Trying to drive me crazy.

BRET
(Pause)

Maybe it *is* her, Mark.

MARK
Her?

BRET

Sandy. You said she threatened to erase your book – and now it's gone!

MARK

But she's – she's dead.

BRET

Is she? They haven't found her body, have they? She *could* be out there.

MARK

Still *alive*? . . . Is it possible?

BRET

Would she do this to you? Fake her death? Plant evidence? Erase your book? To hurt you?

MARK

I never knew what she was really like, Bret. I never knew what she was capable of until it was too late!

BRET

What did you do that she could hate you so much?

MARK

All I did was love you. . . . I never loved her. She threatened to erase my entire book unless I left you. But I never could leave you! She wanted me to feel the same pain she felt. Well, I feel the pain!

BRET

Mark -- if Sandy really is alive, then there's nothing to prove. You're innocent.

MARK

The truth didn't stop Craig when he beat that confession out of Henry White. Now Craig is going to hound me until I crack, until he ties a knot around my neck, no matter what I did!

BRET

(With realization, picking up the nightgown)

When Detective Craig was here before, he wanted me to wear this.

MARK

He -- what?

BRET

To trap you.

MARK

Trap me? . . . That bastard! He wanted to see you dressed in that nightgown!

BRET

(Noticing the nightgown has been ripped)

Mark!

(MARK *takes the nightgown from* HER, *looks at it, and sees it's been cut)*

MARK

(With realization)

Craig! *He* sent you that nightgown! He's been framing me all along! Trying to drive me to confess!

BRET

He said others would die if I didn't go through with his plan. Just like Sandy died. Just like -- Gill . . .

MARK

He said Gill was dead? How can he know that Gill's dead?

BRET

(With realization)

How could he be so certain? About Sandy? About Gill? How could he *know* unless . . . unless . . .

MARK

Unless what?

BRET

Unless he killed them. Oh, God!

(Breaking down)

Gill's not really dead! She's not! She can't be!

MARK

(Moving to comfort HER*)*

Bret – I'm here.

BRET

(Allowing HIM *to hold* HER*)*

If Gill's dead, it's my fault!

MARK

If only we'd stayed together, none of this would have happened. Sandy meant nothing to me, and you – everything. You still mean everything.

*(**BRET** removes herself from **MARK'S** embrace)*

You've always been the one safe part of my life. . . . I need to feel there's still some hope for us. . . .

(HE *reaches for* HER)

BRET
(Avoiding HIS *touch)*
Mark . . .

MARK
Sandy never really has gone, has she? . . . Even now -- I feel her. Between us.

ERIC
(Entering)
Bret! They just found a woman's body buried in Cascadilla Gorge.

BRET
A -- body? Is it . . . is it -- Gill?

ERIC
There's been no identification.

BRET
He killed her! Detective Craig killed Gill!

ERIC
You think -- Craig . . .?

MARK
There's evidence he may have.

ERIC
We don't know that Craig did anything. We don't even know if that body is Gill. We don't *know* anything.

*(***BRET*** gets her parka)*
What are you doing?

BRET
I'm going to Cascadilla Gorge -- or the police station -- or wherever they've taken her. I've got to find out if it's Gill.

MARK
There's nothing you can do now, Bret.

BRET
But I have to do something!

MARK
I'll go with you then.

ERIC
(To **BRET***)*
No. If it is Gill, you shouldn't see her like that.
(To **MARK***)*
Why don't you go by yourself, Mark. Check it out.

MARK

And what about you? Staying here, are you? Where you're so obviously welcome.

BRET

Mark!

MARK

Don't worry, I'm leaving.

(MARK crosses to the DR door, then pauses)

Bret – it didn't have to turn out this way.

(HE exits DR, closing the door open.

BRET

(Distraught)

I should never have come here. Should never have asked Gill to stay. Should never have believed Craig.

ERIC

It's not your fault. . . . Look, I'm going to check out what's happening at the gorge. If I have to, I'll go to the police station.

BRET

I'll come with you.

ERIC

No. That wouldn't be a good idea.

BRET

But . . .

ERIC

Bret -- you can't change anything that's happened. It's too late. . . . I want you to stay here, so I'll know where you'll be. . . . Promise me?

BRET

I -- promise.

ERIC

I want you to lock yourself in my apartment. I'm not sure about Craig -- or anyone else right now. I think it would be safer.

(HE hands HER a key)

Here's the key to my place. I'll knock like this --

(HE knocks quickly twice, pause, once, pause, quickly twice)

And you can let me in when I get back.

BRET

All right.

ERIC

Promise me you'll stay there.

BRET

I promise.

> (**ERIC** *gives* HER *a gentle kiss*)

ERIC

> (*As* HE *exits* DR)

I'll be back as soon as I can.

> (**BRET** *locks the door* DR, *then crosses to the desk and dials a number.*
>
> (*Silently, the mirror-door opens.* **HAROLD** *steps into the apartment. He has a bleeding wound on his forehead. He approaches* **BRET**. *She remains unaware of his approach*)

BRET

I want to speak to someone about . . .

> (**HAROLD** *rips the phone cord out of the wall, then grabs* **BRET** *from behind, putting his hand over her mouth*)

HAROLD

Don't scream, Miss Conway.

> (**BRET** *struggles under his grip, but is unable to break free*)

Stop fighting. I don't want to hurt you, but I will if I have to.

> (**BRET** *stands still, very tense*)

That's better. . . . Now, I'm going to take my hand away, so promise me you won't scream.

> (*When* **BRET** *nods affirmatively,* **HAROLD** *slowly removes his hand*)

BRET

What do you want?

HAROLD

Not what you think. Not what any of you think. Move over there.

> (*HE shoves* HER *in the direction of the mirror-door*)

BRET

The mirror! You watched all of us through that mirror!

HAROLD

And I saw too much.

BRET

Where's Gill?

HAROLD

She's dead. I've seen that.

BRET

You killed her! And Sandy!

HAROLD

No! A killer came here -- inside my walls. He took them from me. I thought of running -- but where would I go? I belong here -- in these walls. It was so -- right -- until *he* came.

BRET

Until who came?

HAROLD

Detective Russell Craig -- snooping around -- spying. He thinks he knows everything.

BRET

(Beginning to move stealthily toward HER *purse)*

Where is he? What have you done to him?

HAROLD

Done to *him*? Look at my face!

BRET

Detective Craig did that to you?

HAROLD

You still don't understand, do you? Craig left that suitcase. I saw him. He took your tape. He wouldn't have protected you. He would have hurt you, if he thought he had to -- to get what he wanted.

BRET

And you're who he wants.

HAROLD

He despises me -- because he's so like me. Waiting in the shadows for the moment when he enters and overpowers them. Stripping away the things they think protect them. But *I'm* not who he wants.

*(**BRET** leaps, attempting to grab up her purse, but **HAROLD** forestalls her, picking up the purse and immediately opening it and pulling out the knife. He points it at **BRET** threateningly)*

I saw you put this knife in here. I told you -- I've seen everything!

*(**BRET** backs away as **HAROLD** continues to approach her)*

And now – it's time for you to see.

BRET

No!

*(**BRET** suddenly bolts for the door, DR, but **HAROLD** catches her by the arm)*

HAROLD

Please don't make me hurt you!

(HAROLD continues to force **BRET** *in the direction of the mirror/door.* **BRET** *backs away in the direction of the easel stool. She suddenly grabs the stool and heaves it at* **HAROLD***, striking him. He drops the knife as he sprawls backward so that he is between* **BRET** *and the door,* DR*)*

BRET

(As SHE *spurts toward the fire escape windows and fumbles to open them)*

Help! . . . Help!

(HAROLD leaps across the room at HER*, grabbing her ankle and tripping her.* HAROLD *pulls her toward him by the ankle.*

(BRET kicks her foot loose, as HAROLD *reaches for, then grabs, the knife. She jumps up and rushes toward the* DR *door with* HAROLD *in pursuit. Just as* **BRET** *reaches the door and opens it,* **MARK** *lunges in from the hallway.* **BRET** *screams)*

　　　　MARK *is dressed as last seen.*

(HAROLD freezes at the sight of **MARK***)*

Mark! He has a knife!

MARK

(Staring at the mirror-door, and then at **HAROLD***)*

You've been spying on us all along! You've seen everything!

HAROLD

(Holding the knife in a threatening manner)

Stay away from me!

(HAROLD suddenly flees toward the mirror-door, but **MARK** *rushes* **HAROLD***, catching him just outside the passageway They struggle.* **MARK** *grabs* **HAROLD'S** *knife hand and stabs* **HAROLD** *in the gut, pulling the knife out as* **HAROLD** *stumbles back just inside the mirror passageway and collapses to the floor. Dazed,* **MARK** *drops the knife on the bedside table)*

BRET

Oh my God! Is he . . . ?

MARK

He's dead. I've killed him.

BRET

(Crossing toward the phone)

Mark, we've got to call the police.

MARK

No, wait! I've got to think this through.

BRET

You were protecting me. It was self-defense. The police will see that.

MARK

Yes – it was Harold – he must have killed them.

BRET

I'm going to call the police.

MARK

Bret! I need to hold you.

(BRET embraces MARK supportively, and he gratefully)

You'll stay with me now, won't you?

BRET

(Pulling away gently)

Mark . . . there's still Sandy.

MARK

Sandy!. . Damn her! You don't know what that woman did to me, Bret! She erased my entire book – that's what she did! And then blackmailed me with the back-ups – said she'd give them to me only if I gave her credit! Only if I left you.

BRET

(Pause)

When did she blackmail you? Your book was erased *tonight* -- wasn't it?

MARK

She tried to ruin me! I had to do something to stop her!

BRET

What did you do?

MARK

(Speaking more to HIMSELF *than to* **BRET** *-- not even looking at her)*

God, what a mess! I just want it to stop. I just want to let it go. I want to — just go. . . . *We* can go now, Bret. *Together.* Like it always should have been.

BRET

Go? Go where?

MARK

Anywhere . . . You wanted me once -- trusted me.

BRET

What have you done to Sandy, Mark?

MARK

It's as if she's risen from the grave to haunt me. . . . Damn her! Damn her to hell! I want to bury her just like Gill!

BRET

Just like Gill?

MARK

Gill knew everything. Just like you do now. . . . You understand what I'm saying, don't you?

BRET

Oh, God! *You* killed Gill!

MARK

I had to. She knew about the book. She would have guessed the rest.

BRET

You killed them both!

(**BRET** *retreats from* **MARK** *as he pursues her, pleading*)

MARK

I had no choice!

BRET

No choice? I wanted to believe you! Every lie! Because I loved you! How could I have loved you?

MARK

It was her fault! Don't you see? Everything was her fault!

BRET

No!

MARK

I killed her so I could save us, but I've still lost everything! All of it! Because of her! It's as if she never died. . . . But Sandy *is* dead.

(**MARK** *picks up the knife from the bedside table and turns to* **BRET**)

Now you're the only one who knows the truth.

BRET

Please, Mark. Put the knife down.

(**BRET** *backs toward the fire escape windows, but* **MARK** *cuts her off.*)

MARK

You don't realize how one misstep can lead into total darkness. One mistake and you've lost your way.

BRET

Mark! Don't do this!

MARK

(Still stalking HER*)*

I never wanted to hurt you. I always loved you.

BRET

Mark! Please stop!

MARK

(Continuing to approach HER*)*

Don't you see? It's too late.

*(***MARK*** *raises his knife, ready to stab* **BRET***, but he is forestalled when he sees the mirror door open. He grabs* **BRET***, holding the knife to her throat as* **CRAIG** *enters.*

(A severed loop of rope remains tied around one of **CRAIG'S** *wrists. His brow is bloody. He is carrying his gun)*

Ah -- Detective Craig. So Bret has become your decoy after all!

CRAIG

(Aiming HIS *gun at* **MARK***)*

Drop the knife!

MARK

It was *you.* You planted everything.

CRAIG

Whatever it takes. Now let her go.

MARK

I can't.

*(***MARK*** *backs toward the open fire escape windows, pulling* **BRET** *along as a shield)*

We belong together – Bret and I.

(To **BRET**)

Isn't that right, my love?

(As they near the easel stand **BRET'S** *hand grasps the glass jar of turpentine)*

ERIC

(Off, knocking loudly at the DR *door)*

Bret! Bret!

BRET

Eric!

MARK

No!

The SOUND *of* **ERIC** *hurling himself against the* DR *door is heard.*

(While **MARK** *is distracted by the sound,* **BRET** *flings the turpentine into* **MARK'S** *eyes.*

(Clawing HIS *eyes,* **MARK** *screams in pain.* **MARK** *sinks to his knees, dropping the knife.*

(Training his gun on **MARK**, **CRAIG** *rushes to* **MARK** *and kicks the knife out of* **MARK'S** *reach.*

(As **CRAIG** *handcuffs* **MARK**, **ERIC** *breaks through the apartment door)*

> **ERIC**

(Hurriedly crossing to **BRET** *to comfort* HER *and draw her away from* **MARK***)*

Bret! I'm here.

(Maintaining his surveillance of **MARK**, **CRAIG** *checks on* **HAROLD**, *confirming he is dead.*

*(***CRAIG** *then crosses to* **MARK** *and hauls him to his feet.* **CRAIG** *stands upstage from* **MARK***)*

> **MARK**

Bret . . .

*(***BRET** *turns to face* **MARK**. **ERIC** *stands behind her)*

I don't know – how it came to this. Please, Bret --

> **BRET**
>
> *(Interrupting)*

No more lies, Mark.

> **MARK**

It wasn't a lie – what we felt – remember – that time at the inn – It's fall – and we're lying there – listening – to the sound of the sea.

> **BRET**

Yes. And you destroyed it all. That's what I'll always remember.

> **CRAIG**

Mark Ryder, I am arresting you for the murder of Gillian Hastings, Harold Lemb, and Sandy Barker.

> *The* SOUND *of the bells from the university clock tower begins to strike midnight.*

(While the bells are heard, **BRET** *and* **MARK** *continue to stare at each other)*

You have the right to remain silent. . . . You have the right . . .

> RAPID FADE *to* BLACK.

END *of the* PLAY

PROPERTY PLOT

Top of show preset:
NEXT TO THE APARTMENT DOOR: A red suitcase (or similarly distinctive suitcase) is next to the apartment door
ABOVE THE DRESSER: A framed print
ON WALL BETWEEN BATHROOM/KITCHENETTE DOOR AND WRITING DESK UR: Framed print
ON WRITING DESK: Word processor, books, papers and writing utensils haphazardly stacked. Some books piled on the floor next to the desk
ON WALL ABOVE DESK: Framed print
ON CONVERTIBLE SOFA DC: A flowery comforter on an unmade bed
ON SIDE TABLE NEXT TO COUCH: A boom box, a small lamp
OVER THE   BACK OF THE STUFFED CHAIR DC: Several shirts, a pair of jeans and a bra
UC: IN FIRE ESCAPE WINDOW: A broken pane of glass near the lock

ON DR PROP TABLE:
HAROLD: A tool belt with a hammer, screwdriver, tape measure and flashlight. A 14"x10"x4"gift-wrapped package with a big red bow and an attached card, containing a sexy full-length, black nightgown
SANDY: A purse containing a rent check

Scene Changes
From I - 1 to I - 2:
STRIKE D: boom box, comforter, all clothes, purse, suitcase, gift box

SET D: tie back curtains, make bed and fold it into couch

STRIKE U: all objects, prints and clothing from and around desk except lamp

SET U: replace simulated broken window with cardboard "pane", vacuum cleaner

ON DR PROP TABLE:
HAROLD: Dust cloth
BRET: Purse

From I - 2 to I - 3:
SET D:
NEAR APARTMENT DOOR: Coat rack; Bret's parka on the coat rack
ON WALLS: Above dresser, charcoal portraits of people with haunting eyes and of some threatening subject matter.
DL NEAR WINDOW ALCOVE: Easel with stretched canvas painting, the painted side not visible to the audience, stool
NEXT TO EASEL: stand with linseed oil jar, turpentine jar containing paint brushes, additional paint brushes, palette with dabs of paint, rag, and a large palette knife.
ON FLOOR NEXT TO EASEL: can of turpentine clearly marked, painting case with various tubes of oil paint, brushes

STRIKE U: vacuum cleaner

SET U:
ON DESK: Telephone/answering machine with tape. Pottery jar holding pens and pencils, a small pad of note paper, and various desk supplies and books, neatly arranged
ABOVE DESK AND ON WALL BETWEEN MIRROR AND BATHROOM / KITCHENETTE DOOR: Charcoal portraits of people with haunting eyes
IN DRESSER DRAWER: Bret's shirt
ON TOP OF DRESSER: A   large tape deck and an assortment of tapes
DC: Neutral colored comforter, folded over back of couch

OUTSIDE DR DOOR: A 42" long by 24" deep by 30" wide wooden trunk (Eric's art trunk)

ON DR PROP TABLE:
HAROLD: A tool belt with a hammer, screwdriver, flashlight and tape measure, a gift-wrapped package with a big white

bow and an attached card, containing a sexy, full-length black nightgown
ERIC: A hammer, chisel and the suitcase in I-1
MARK: Briefcase
GILL: Large, distinctive purse containing wine bottle and corkscrew

ON UR PROP TABLE:
BRET: Two wineglasses

ON UL PROP TABLE:
CRAIG: Police badge

From I - 3 to I - 4
OUTSIDE DR DOOR: Two large suitcases adorned w/international
stickers and filled w/an assortment of brightly colored women's clothing
ON DR PROP TABLE:
GILL: Purse
MARK: Briefcase
BRET: Robe

STRIKE: Wine bottle and glasses

Intermission Preset
GILL'S purse is on the floor next to the couch, DC. GILL'S coat is where she left it at the end of Act One. The bedside lamp and the black nightgown are on the floor near the couch bed.

ON DR PROP TABLE:
HAROLD: Tool belt with hammer, screwdriver, flashlight and tape measure
BRET: Purse, parka

OUTSIDE DR ENTRANCE:
ERIC: Art trunk

From II - 1 to II - 2

SET:
DC: Couch/bed is made into a couch
ON UR DESK: Bret's purse

ON DR PROP TABLE:
MARK: Xeroxed copies of newspaper clippings in a folder
CRAIG: Sandy's purse from I-1

ON UR PROP TABLE:
BRET: Large kitchen knife

ON UC PROP TABLE:
CRAIG: Gill's coat and her purse containing a wallet, handgun, rope

ON UL PROP TABLE:
CRAIG/FIGURE: Handgun, Flashlight

From II - 2 to II - 3
SET:
UC: Close mirror door; return lamp to upright position, remove Gill's purse and coat

ON DR PROP TABLE:
BRET: Purse containing large kitchen knife.

BIOGRAPHICAL NOTES

Jan Henson Dow, **Robert Schroeder**, and **Shannon Michal Dow** have won numerous playwriting competitions, including an NBC "New Voices" award, and their plays and musicals are staged nationally. Their plays have been published by Samuel French and Popular Play Service.

Jan Henson Dow, as a Professor at Western Connecticut State University, directed the Playwriting Workshops, and co-produced Western's Festival of New Plays. She has been the recipient of a number of playwriting grants, as well as production grants for the new play festival.

Ms. Dow received her M.A. from the University of North Carolina at Chapel Hill, and her B.A. from Indiana University. Her articles and poems have appeared in such publications as *The New York Times, The Dramatists Guild Quarterly, Kansas Quarterly, Indiana Review, Connecticut Review,* and *Piedmont Literary Review.*

Robert Schroeder, a graduate of Ohio State University, was on the staff of *The Dramatists Guild Quarterly* and of the Dodd-Mead *Best Plays* reference annuals. His reviews and theater commentaries also appeared in *The Nation, Commonweal, New York,* and other periodicals. His anthology *The New Underground Theater* was published by Bantam Books, and he was among the contributors to *Playwrights, Lyricists, and Composers on Theater*, a Dodd-Mead hardcover. His children's musical, *Tom Thumb*, toured professionally.

Shannon Michal Dow has been a feature writer and editor, and a film and theater reviewer. She has an M.S. in Education and currently is an English teacher and is working on a variety of writing and artistic projects.

www.ingramcontent.com/pod-product-compliance
Lightning Source LLC
Chambersburg PA
CBHW060039040426
42331CB00032B/1447